LIVING IN THE LIGHT OF ETERNITY

LIVING IN THE LIGHT OF ETERNITY

STACY & PAULA RINEHART

The Navigators is an international, evangelical Christian organisation. Jesus Christ gave his followers the Great Commission to go and make disciples (Matthew 28:19). The aim of The Navigators is to help fulfil that commission by multiplying labourers for Christ in every nation.
NavPress is the publishing ministry of The Navigators. NavPress publications are tools to help Christians grow. Although publications alone cannot make disciples or change lives, they can help believers learn biblical discipleship, and apply what they learn to their lives and ministries.

This edition issued by special arrangement with NavPress, a ministry of The Navigators, U.S.A. Original title LIVING IN LIGHT OF ETERNITY.

First U.K. edition published by The Navigators Great Britain in 1987.

ISBN: 0 948188 30 8.

Printed in Great Britain.

The Navigators
Tregaron House
27 High Street
New Malden
Surrey KT3 4BY
Tel:(01) 942 2211

Contents

Authors

Stacy Rinehart holds a Doctor of Ministry degree from Trinity Evangelical Divinity School and a Master of Theology degree from Dallas Theological Seminary. He is the director of the Leadership Development Institute at Glen Eyrie in Colorado Springs, Colorado. Previously he served as the Navigator representative in Tulsa, Oklahoma. He also directed the Navigator student ministry at Oklahoma State University. Stacy came into contact with The Navigators at Fort Benning, Georgia, while serving as an officer in the U.S. Army.

Paula Rinehart is a graduate of the University of Tennessee, where she was involved with The Navigators.

Stacy and Paula are the authors of the award-winning NavPress book *Choices*. They live in Colorado Springs with their two children, Allison and Brady.

To
Allison and Brady,
whose lives give us
joy in the present
and
hope for the future.

We fix our eyes not on what is
seen, but on what is unseen. For
what is seen is temporary, but
what is unseen is eternal.

2 Corinthians 4:18

Preface

What is it that transforms an ordinary person into someone with extraordinary impact in his respective arena of influence? We believe the missing link is one of *vision*, the ability to see what is unseen, to weigh life's various options on the scales of eternity. As creatures made in the image of God, designed for immortality, we need an eternal perspective to determine what really matters in life.

For almost fifteen years now we have been engaged in helping people cross the invisible hurdles of spiritual growth. We have known that sharp, jabbing discomfort of tripping across a few of those hurdles ourselves. Perhaps our greatest hurdle has been determining the true meaning of success.

This book has grown from our contact with ordinary people who have struggled to lift personal applications right off their Bible study pages, to wear them into the everyday world of office buildings and department store closeouts. It is the fruit of helping couples with two incomes think through lifestyle choices they face—and helping college graduates who have left the campus whirlwind of studies and social experiences to face the competitive, workaday rush to "get ahead."

It is our conviction that all the religious activity, our Bible study, and personal devotions must be a preparation, not a substitution, for dealing with the pivotal kinds of choices facing all of us: What am I giving my life to? Do my goals, ambitions, and values reflect the beliefs I espouse? How much of what I consider important does God consider valuable in light of eternity?

These are perhaps the most crucial issues in a modern Christian's life. Allowing these questions to go unexplored may leave you drowning in the shallows of time and space when you could be buoyed up by the depths of eternity.

If you sense the pressure of the world's temporal mind-set, if you long for the integration of seeing life from a larger perspective, if you desire a life of spiritual vitality, we urge you to read on.

1
A Glimpse of Eternity

> We should all be concerned about the future because we will have to spend the rest of our lives there.
>
> *Charles Kettering*

In the early dawn of a promising October Sunday in 1983, more than two hundred Marines slept undisturbed in their barracks next to Lebanon's Beirut International Airport. Suddenly and without warning, a truck loaded with dynamite entered the compound. The driver smiled as he drove past the guards, then accelerated, took aim, and crashed into the barrack's lobby. In the tremendous explosion that followed, the building collapsed, killing or wounding many of the Marines inside and producing the worst disaster for the U.S. Armed Forces since the end of the Vietnam War.

More than hatred of his enemy, however, motivated this terrorist driver's suicide mission. Inbred into his thinking was the mistaken conviction that dying in service to his cause bought immortality and assured eternal reward.

Throughout the course of history, man has embraced a persistent sense of immortality. The ancient Greeks put forth the idea that men could produce words and deeds that would survive their physical existence. All that would be left of a person was the imperishable traces of his former existence.

Modern man continues the search for reality beyond this world. The well-known astronomer and author Carl Sagan writes of such a quest:

> The surface of the Earth is the shore of the cosmic ocean. From it we have learned most of what we know. Recently, we have waded a little out to sea, enough to dampen our toes or, at most, wet our ankles. The water seems inviting. The ocean calls. Some part of our being knows this is from where we came. We long to return.[1]

The implication is that if we could "return," we would find our origin, which would help us shape our future.

This hunger for something more, this search for the larger tapestry that will make sense of our frayed individual strands, brings us face-to-face with a compelling choice between two very different visions of life. We must answer whether death is the end of the story or simply the introduction to a new and expanded chapter. "Do the tangled paths through the forest of life lead to the golden castle or over the cliff and into the abyss? Is death a door or a hole?"[2] The stakes are high, for our view of a future life beyond death in large measure shapes our outlook on the present life.

A great hope

Christianity is the audacious assertion that our longing for roots and an eternal destiny can be realized in a person. "The Word became flesh, and dwelt among us" (John 1:14) is the message we celebrate at Christmas—a proclamation reminding us that the Immortal took the form of the mortal so that we, in turn, might someday lay aside the temporal and don the imperishable.

For the Christian, eternal life is far more than the vague hope of future generations who will carry our genes, or the ripples of our individual lives in the ocean of time (as philosophers have asserted from time immemorial). Rather, eternal life is the very essence of our being brought back into true union with the One who created us. When Jesus said, "I go to prepare a place for you . . . that where I am, there you may be also" (John 14:2-3), He spoke of a future event we have come to call "the blessed hope" (Titus 2:13). The modern connotation of hope as a vague kind of wishing, however, would be a misnomer. Christ spoke this promise of a heavenly future as a statement of certain fact.

As surely as we are mortally limited in time and space now, someday we will be eternally with God. Yet Scripture has a strange way of superimposing the glorious future on the imperfect present, describing them as complementary parts of a larger reality. The author of Hebrews speaks of the present time frame when he says, "You have been allowed to approach the true Mount Zion, the city of the living God, the heavenly Jerusalem. You have drawn near to the countless angelic army. . . . You have drawn near to God, the judge of all . . ." (Hebrews 12:22-23, PH). God intends for us to relate the future eternal realm to our lives in the present.

As Peter caught sight of the reality of an eternal dimension, he asked a question of direct relevance to us: Since we know that God has an eternal plan and purpose for us, what kind of people should we be? (2 Peter 3:11). How should the reality of endless life into the future influence the way we live now?

Dedicated believers throughout the ages have lived in the shadow of this profoundly relevant question. Abraham left his country and his kindred for the land God would show him. Why? Because he desired "a better country, that is a heavenly one." And Moses, "seeing Him who is unseen," turned his back on the wealth and refinement of Egypt to lead a collection of grumbling Hebrews into the Promised Land. He preferred a part in God's eternal purposes rather than the enjoyment of Egypt's "passing pleasures." For both Abraham and Moses, the values of the eternal determined the choices in the here and now (Hebrews 11:8-27).

To see this life in light of the life to come, to accept eternity as the dominant reality, is to have what we call an *eternal perspective.* Four centuries ago, Martin Luther said that on his calendar there were but two days: "Today and That Day." He recognized that all the days of his earthly existence were preparation for that momentous day when he would stand before God in eternity and give an account for his life.

Wherever the Kingdom of God has advanced, it's been because of men and women who so highly appraise the eternal that they willingly sacrifice the temporal and perishable. A martyred twentieth-century missionary, Jim Elliot, said, "I am willing that my house on earth be emptier [if only] His house be fuller." Elliot expressed the contrast of the temporal and the eternal well when he said, "He is no fool who gives away what he cannot keep, to gain what he cannot lose."[3]

In a general sense, we could compare the concept of an eternal perspective to the psychological phrase "deferred gratification," or the accountant's idea of "deferred compensation." In each case it means living with short-term costs in order to reap long-term gains. An eternal perspective will affect our values, priorities, and outlook on life as we make decisions about the immediate in light of the ultimate.

Recapturing the glory

But orienting our lives for the deeper reality of God's Kingdom, living now in light of eternity, is not a posture we readily assume, especially in our modern age. Heaven often seems like a spiritual version of an outer space movie—so immensely far removed from the world of split-levels and fast food. We sometimes echo Thoreau, who wanted to take life "one world at a time."

Medieval man was apparently more adept than modern man at relating his present life to the hope of heaven. Peter Kreeft describes the perspective of medieval man:

> Earth was Heaven's womb, Heaven's nursery, Heaven's dress rehearsal. Heaven was the meaning of the earth. . . . Medieval man was still his Father's child, however prodigal, and his world was meaningful because it was "my Father's world" and he believed his Father's promise to take him home after death. This confidence towards death gave him a confidence towards life, for life's road led somewhere.[4]

Our sense of heavenly glory, however, is undermined by the illusion that things are real and permanent simply because we can touch, see, or smell them. The tangible, the concrete, the material, so captivate us that we fail to look beyond them. We become the child who just can't get past the candy the Easter bunny left him long enough to really appreciate the impact of the true Easter message: that God conquered death.

Yet in the midst of all the comfortable and familiar, there is a gnawing, unsettled feeling reminding us that there is more. Where does that feeling come from? From God. "He has . . . set eternity in [our] hearts" (Ecclesiastes 3:11). C.S. Lewis described how that innate sense of eternity prompts our desires:

> All the things that have ever deeply possessed your soul have been but hints of [heaven]—tantalising glimpses, promises never quite fulfilled, echoes that died away just as they caught your ear. . . . If I find in myself a desire which no experience in this world can satisfy, the most probable explanation is that I was made for another world. . . . Probably earthly pleasures were never meant to satisfy it, but only to arouse it, to suggest the real thing.[5]

Even secular writer and thinker Aldous Huxley admitted, "Sooner or later one asks even of Shakespeare, even of Beethoven, 'Is that all?'"

Dealing with distortion

Before we can develop a taste for the eternal, we must deal with our misconceptions about heaven and eternity.

Perhaps the chief misconception is the mistaken idea that living now in light of the future, or seeing life with an eternal perspective, is spiritual escapism. In other words, all this talk of heaven is perceived as a cowardly, ostrich-like means of shirking responsibility here and now by people who are so heavenly minded they're no earthly good.

Certainly there are some Christians who use eternity as an excuse to treat this life as a holding tank, a waiting room, a picnic in the park before the Great Event. But they are not Christians who have carefully read their Bibles or their history books.

William Wilberforce, a Christian parliamentarian and abolitionist leader of the 1800s, devoted nearly fifty years of his life to abolishing the slave trade in England. Why? Because he saw slaves as people of eternal worth and slavery as an affront to God's eternal truth.

> The Apostles themselves, who set on foot the conversion of the Roman Empire, the great men who built up the Middle Ages, the English Evangelicals who abolished the Slave Trade, all left their mark on Earth, precisely because their minds were occupied with Heaven. It is since Christians have largely ceased to think of the other world that they have become so ineffective in this.[6]

The people who have made the greatest impact for Christ in this world have lived according to a perspective encompassing both time and eternity. God created both this world and heaven to reflect His glory. Our purpose in life is to establish a beachhead of His Kingdom here and now.

The question of escapism really depends on how big you consider reality to be. Percentages don't apply, of course, but for the sake of argument, if we assume that over ninety-nine percent of our existence will be in heaven, it doesn't make sense to live as though the present were all-important. "The shape into which we shape ourselves now is the shape of our eternal selves; only the size (that is, the dimension) is changed."[7] Not to have prepared for that eternal dimension would be escapism in the truest sense of the term.

Yahweh, the great "I AM" who exists throughout all eternity, created us to fellowship with Him. Adam and Eve knew Him in the totally integrated world of the Garden of Eden, which suffered no false distinctions between the temporal and the eternal. The Fall eclipsed God's intentions. Death entered, locking man out of God's direct presence and into a world where the eternal dimension is veiled—very much among us and yet just out of reach.

We live with a gnawing dissatisfaction we cannot quite name, a mysterious sense of being made for another world. When we celebrate the Lord's Table, we stand for a moment outside of time, seeing the Lamb who was slain before the foundation of the world, who shed His blood on Golgotha, who will come again in glory.

To live in the light of true reality, then, we must live now in the shadow of the glory we will someday inhabit. The King is preparing His wedding feast; the Bridegroom awaits. The hosts of heaven look on. It is thus our challenge to live now in light of the words we will say then: "Let us rejoice and be glad and give the glory to Him, for the marriage of the Lamb has come and His bride has made herself ready" (Revelation 19:7).

His bride has made herself ready. Can we say that of ourselves? Do our eyes look toward the sure and purifying gaze of the Bridegroom? Do our ears heed His compelling voice? Are our hearts prepared with worship that will spring forth in His presence when we "cry aloud and shout for joy . . . for great in [our] midst is the Holy One of Israel"? (Isaiah 12:6).

Though we now catch only a glimpse of eternity through a glass darkly, on that Day we will see the Eternal One clearly just as He is. "And every one who has this hope fixed on Him purifies himself, just as He is pure" (1 John 3:3).

Notes

1. Carl Sagan, *Cosmos* (New York: Random House, 1980), page 5.
2. Peter Kreeft, *Everything You Ever Wanted to Know About Heaven* (San Francisco: Harper & Row, 1982), page 3.
3. Elisabeth Elliot, *Shadow of the Almighty* (Grand Rapids: Zondervan, 1958), page 160.
4. Peter Kreeft, *Everything*, pages 3-4.
5. C.S. Lewis, *The Problem of Pain* (New York: MacMillan, 1962), page 134; C.S. Lewis, *Mere Christianity* (New York: MacMillan, 1943), page 120.
6. C.S. Lewis, *Mere Christianity*, page 118.
7. Peter Kreeft, *Everything*, page 10.

2
Caught Between Two Worlds

Beware what you set your heart upon,
for it surely shall be yours.

Amy Carmichael

As Wang Lung sifted the soft dirt between his fingers, he noticed how his sweat glistened in faint beads upon his arms. Out of the corner of his eye he could see Olan patiently tilling up one small patch of ground after another, her middle heavy with child. Although Olan was hardly beautiful, Wang Lung knew that this woman who had borne his children and labored through the years beside him was rare indeed.

When the rains and the harvest cooperated, Wang Lung and Olan ate; when the crops failed, they went hungry. But Olan never complained. In the fields she worked as hard as any man. At home it was her pleasure to wait on her husband and children.

For years Wang Lung and his wife eked out a life of bare subsistence from the landowner's soil. Then a handful of fateful circumstances totally changed their lot. Olan's quick thinking and ingenuity enabled them to buy their own small plot of land.

After years of careful cultivation and good fortune, Wang Lung himself became a wealthy landowner, able to buy the labor of others. But in this time of leisure and self-satisfaction, his eyes turned elsewhere.

The wife of his youth no longer aroused his affection, still less his desire. Gradually his persistent steps wore a path to the house of a slender girl, whose fingernails were stained with lotus petals. Every night he made forays of pleasure to her house; every morning he emerged more determined to return.

After months of such inconvenience, Wang Lung reasoned to himself, "I am a wealthy man with servants that do as I bid them. They will build a special room onto my house and I will move this girl and her servant there under my own roof."

Olan refused to feed her husband's mistress or to even acknowledge her presence. The Chinese have a saying that no house is large enough for two women. Wang Lung's home was never again the same. This is just a small tragic part of Pearl Buck's classic story of the Chinese peasant family in *The Good Earth.*

Relationships in the visible world can often reveal to us the deeper truths of the invisible one.

In a strange way, this simple Chinese peasant family pictures for us the adultery of robbing the Lord of our first love. God becomes the jilted lover whose faithfulness is bartered on the altar of cheap substitutes. That exchange is the essence of what we commonly call worldliness.

We live with the paradox of knowing that although we are destined for the world to come, we must still live in *this* world. We feel its insistent tug. That pithy phrase, "Christians should be in the world but not of it," is much easier to say than to live out.

In an effort to avoid the world and ensure spirituality pure and undefiled, people throughout the ages have devised drastic escape measures. Simeon the Stylite, for instance, was an ascetic who chose to live atop a pillar for thirty years, believing that whatever starved the body fed the soul. Others retreated to monasteries to protect their faith from a corrupt world.

Living as a desert hermit, an ascetic on a pillar, or a cloistered monk in order to escape the world would not be an unreasonable solution . . . if it worked. History reveals, however, that it was much easier to get the monk out of the world than the world out of the monk. The Fall planted seeds of potential for worldliness in each of our hearts—seeds that are ready to bloom into a rampant weed patch of carnality wherever we go.

Being different for the right reasons

We may not have been caught up into the third heaven or heard words inexpressible, as Paul intimated about himself (2 Corinthians 12:2-4). But our glimpse of eternity in Christ and in the Word is sufficient motivation to live distinctively. The early Christians lived so differently from the neighboring Jews and pagans that they were called "the third race." How should our lives reflect that deeper reality we have placed our hope in? In what ways should our lives be different?

A close study of the life of Jesus Christ reveals someone who loved the world without losing any aspect of His holiness. He was holy, undefiled, totally separate from sin. Yet He willingly accepted the label of friend to publicans and prostitutes. Not taking advantage of the position that was rightfully His, Jesus washed the feet of those who would fail Him in His darkest hours. He refused to be bound by the legalistic taboos of a false spirituality. Because He was holy, He expressed His love for the world in a life of genuine humility.

The Apostle John gave perhaps the most concise, insightful definition of worldliness in his first letter: "Do not love the world, nor the things in the world. . . . For all that is in the world, the lust of the flesh and the lust of the eyes and the boastful pride of life, is not from the Father, but is from the world" (1 John 2:15-16). Vernon Grounds points out that these three categories cover the whole spectrum of worldliness. The lust of the flesh is *sensualism*—a selfish, excessive gratification of our physical nature. The lust of the eyes is *materialism*—grappling for things we want but don't really need. And the boastful pride of life is *egotism*—"the self-centered hankering to inflate our own little reputations."[1]

The enemy always seeks to sidetrack us from dealing with these deeper issues of motives, attitudes, and values. Since our earliest days, Christians have persisted in defining worldliness by an external code of dos and don'ts. Paul chastised the Colossians for evaluating their spirituality by the worldly standards of what they ate, handled, or touched. He tackled the Galatians on the issue of circumcision and the Romans for quibbling over how they kept the Sabbath.

Christ spoke of straining out a gnat and swallowing a camel (Matthew 23:24), meaning that we sometimes make major issues of secondary concerns. In one breath we denounce dancing and movies, and in the next we share questionable, derogatory information about another brother. Yet the Bible is silent on the first two subjects and scathing on the latter. What eats away at our spiritual life is not the cultural trivia we haggle over, but the covert presence of attitudes like jealousy, pride, loving the life of luxury, or loving the approval of man.

Worldly attitudes can dress themselves in deceptively spiritual garb. When I was in seminary, a young man hungry for knowledge, I used to savor and then mentally dissect some of our chapel messages. At first, I applauded my newly sharpened ability to discern truth from error, to detect the waddle of a poorly turned phrase. Then I faced my analytical tendency for what it was: mostly an effort to prop up my own speaking insecurities, which had sprung from my hidden envy of others' spiritual gifts. These negative attitudes were just as worldly as longing for a car that out-performs the neighbor's—but much more difficult to label as such.

Similarly, it was once my job to organize a home Bible study for a group of Christians who lived in a Texas-style affluent suburb—affluent, that is, except for one street of very average, ordinary homes. I asked a woman who lived on the "average" street if she would be willing to have the group meet once in her home. She hesitated, floundered, and then finally admitted her true feelings. "I'd like to do that," she said, "but I just don't feel I can have this group in our house until I've redecorated or at least gotten new carpet. Our house is nothing compared to theirs."

This woman would be totally innocent of any item found on the traditional laundry lists of worldly activities. Yet it is this deeper form of bondage, which adopts a worldly measurement of personal worth, that is most characteristic of the spirit of our age. God longs to liberate us from this mind-set of the world, or, as the Apostle Peter says, "from [the] futile way of life inherited from [our] forefathers" (1 Peter 1:18).

Worldliness and idolatry

The tendency to combine a worldly mind-set and values with God's truth produces a spiritual hybrid known in the Old Testament as *idolatry*. When Daniel and his friends were carted off to Babylon, they were offered meat that had been sacrificed to idols and were given Babylonian names containing the name of a heathen god. No one sought to persuade them to openly deny Yahweh, but rather to blend the pagan and the spiritual together, to assign the God of heaven limited lordship, to live as though He were like any other god.

The history of Israel is one long story of how the chosen people chased after the gods of their age. Isaiah used some embarrassingly descriptive language to describe that trek. He called the people of Israel rebellious sons, stubborn asses, forgetful oxen, harlots and prostitutes—words "designed to sting people into shocked awareness [that they] have forgotten *who they are and to whom they rightly belong*."[2]

This same kind of effort to accommodate faith to a warped culture compromises the integrity of the Christian message and confuses the onlooking, unbelieving world. We often blend in, not as a means to identify with people and gain a platform for the gospel, but in order to escape criticism, to avoid making ripples, to protect our own hide. "Our failure commonly arises from our ability to exude only odors that are neither a stench nor a perfume. We are too bland, too insipid."[3]

We both try, periodically, to compare our lives objectively with the lives of our nonChristian friends. Are our values and goals in life markedly different from theirs? Does the use of our time, money, and emotional energy reflect that difference? If not, we know that we have begun to fade into the secular landscape, paying homage to other gods.

In the Scripture, idolatry is equated with its result: *futility*. Some of Samuel's last words to the nation of Israel were, "You must not turn aside, for then you would go after futile things which can not profit or deliver, because they are futile" (1 Samuel 12:21). Since they are only a mirage, a shadow of what we truly long for, these futile pursuits cannot sustain us in the grittier moments of life.

One of the most graphic illustrations of this futility is Charles Colson's description of what his life was like before he met Christ.

> I had arrived at everything I had ever dreamed about as a kid. I was 41 years old, had a healthy six-figure law practice, clients waiting at the door, a yacht in Chesapeake Bay, a limousine and driver, was a friend of the President, and had all kinds of people working for me and others dying to come into my firm. And I never felt more rotten in my life.[4]

Deep down inside, most of us realize that the world offers only fool's gold. But it helps to hear that message from someone who has actually sampled the world's success and found it tasteless—someone other than a preacher or an Old Testament prophet.

To turn aside and go after cultural golden cows always negates a person's profession of viable faith. God reminded His people through Amos, "I hate, I reject your festivals, nor do I delight in your solemn assemblies" (Amos 5:21). In other words, "Don't worry Me with your celebrations when the loyalty and affection of your heart is split."

An issue of the heart

Our hearts are like Wang Lung's home: They are simply not large enough for more than one true loyalty and love at a time. We need to avoid the tug of this world by making Christ and His Kingdom the center of our lives, at the same time putting guards on sentry duty to watch for rivals to His lordship.

Unless we actively make Christ preeminent, our hearts will drift, inevitably following after the gods of this world. One of Amy Carmichael's favorite quotes was, "Beware what you set your heart upon, for it surely shall be yours."[5] We face the same danger as those of Jeremiah's day, who "walked after emptiness and became empty" (Jeremiah 2:5). We are invariably transformed into the likeness of whatever we worship—either the living God or some cheap substitute.

What ensnares a person's heart and affection away from God differs for each of us. Resisting the urge to check ourselves by some external, universal list, we must give the Holy Spirit freedom to put His finger on *whatever* causes us to drift. One indication of that digression, according to James, is a habitual series of conflicts with others. To what degree do those quarrels reflect a denied pleasure or a thwarted lust, some frustrated effort to experience fulfillment as the world defines it? (James 4:1-6).

To live in light of eternity is to take the posture of a runner who is so intent on finishing the race, on following Christ, that all the unnecessary clutter drops off from lack of interest and use. The scriptural model is not one of retreating from this world but that of actively advancing toward another. Like Abraham, who best demonstrated the demeanor of someone "just passing through," we must set our eyes on a better country, on an inheritance that is imperishable and undefiled. As displaced persons in an alien culture, we, like Daniel, can make our lives a statement of God's power in a corrupt world.

Once when the Cleveland Symphony was performing *The Magic Flute* by Mozart, an electrical storm caused the lights to go out. Undaunted by the difficulties, the members of the orchestra knew the music so well that they completed the performance in the dark. At the end of the performance, the audience burst into thunderous applause, and a stagehand illuminated the orchestra and conductor with a flashlight so that they could take their bows.

It is much the same in the spiritual realm. If you know the Master, you can play His music even in the dark. You can live a holy life in an unholy realm. When caught between two worlds, the secret is to develop a mind-set that sees beyond the style of this world to the substance of the next.

Notes

1. Vernon C. Grounds, "Loving the World: Rightly or

Wrongly," *Christianity Today* (April 1980), pages 19-21.

2. John White, *The Golden Cow* (Downers Grove: InterVarsity, 1979), page 19.
3. John White, *Flirting With the World* (Wheaton: Harold Shaw, 1982), page 21.
4. From an interview with Charles Colson in *Christianity Today* (September 1983), pages 12-16.
5. Amy Carmichael, *Gold by Moonlight* (Ft. Washington: Christian Literature Crusade, 1935, reprinted 1952), page 161.

3
Of Value to God

> The meaning of existence is to preserve unspoiled, undisturbed, and undistorted the image of eternity with which each person is born. Like a silver moon in a calm, still pond.
>
> *Aleksandr Solzhenitsyn*

On a clear night we gaze into the heavens, which the psalmist tells us are "the work of [God's] fingers" (Psalm 8:3). Awed by a myriad of stars punctuating a vast velvet blackness, we marvel at the expanse of His handiwork.

But we turn from such a spectacular view to the person standing beside us and somehow overlook that it is *he* who represents the zenith, the crown of creation. God has made him in His very image. For his redemption, for his restoration, God bared His strong right arm to accomplish the work of salvation. "The LORD has bared His holy arm in the sight of all the nations; that all the ends of the earth may see the salvation of our God" (Isaiah 52:10). God saved us at such great effort and cost that, by comparison, fashioning galaxies was mere finger play.

For God so loved the world, a world filled with people, that He gave. The gift of His Son is the proof of His love and an assessment of our worth. We cannot follow in His steps without acquiring this kind of heart for people.

The Master Craftsman

In the Genesis account of creation, we read about how God speaks whole worlds into existence. All that lives in the oceans, dwells upon the land, or flies above it came forth at His command.

In the second chapter, which focuses on the creation of man, it is as though the Director stops and steps onto the stage. God Himself, we are told, took the dust of the ground, formed a man, and breathed life into him. With that act, He separated us from all the rest of creation. Or, as the psalmist explains of man, "Thou hast made him a little lower than God, and dost crown him with glory and majesty" (Psalm 8:5). God bestowed on man a measure of His own glory. In some refracted way, we each possess His image.

But the effect of sin has been to so mar and tarnish God's image in us that we hardly recognize its presence. The effect of evil on a good creation is always one of *undoing* it.

Christ's victory on the Cross placed within our reach the potential to recover what we lost in the Fall and to share, once again, His glory. Now in Christ, as we behold the glory of the Lord in the mirror of His Word, we "are being transformed into the same image from glory to glory" (2 Corinthians 3:18). It is as though we have come almost full circle, with a new, Eden-like perspective. T.S. Eliot put this concept to sublime poetry in some lines from his *Four Quartets*:

> We shall not cease from exploration
> And the end of all our exploring
> Will be to arrive where we started
> And know the place for the first time.

God made us for an eternal purpose. His future plans are the offspring of His original intent. If eternity's values would dictate our own, then seeing God's image restored in others' lives, as well as in ours, will be our paramount concern. But first, we must be able to recognize that God's image is indeed present, with all its hopeful potential, in ourselves and in the people around us.

To see one's eternal identity

Somewhere under our grasping and greed, amid the selfishness and proud autonomy, exists that aspect of ourselves on which the image of God is indelibly imprinted. British novelist Charles Williams called this our "eternal identity." To be able to see such an eternal uniqueness in other people, is, as Elisabeth Elliot said, "a special gift of vision, the power to see for a little while what God meant when He made that person."[1]

It is a comforting thought to realize that God sees us in light of what we become in Him. When Jesus first met Peter, He said, "You are Simon . . .

you shall be called Cephas" (John 1:42). He saw Peter not as the impetuous, unreliable fisherman, but as the bold, sure leader—"the Rock" that he would become.

With our limited human perspective, however, we easily lose sight of a person's untapped potential in Christ. D.L. Moody was an unordained layman who preached to throngs of people in North America and Europe. A former shoe salesman, he became one of the most effective Christian leaders of the nineteenth century.

In Moody's early years, though, hardly anyone foresaw what God would do through his life. Moody's personal appearance was unimpressive. His manner was rough and his speech, at points, was stuttering and unintelligible. Unable to see beyond his personal limitations, the committee rejected his first application for church membership, saying he was "unlikely ever to become a Christian of clear and decided views of Gospel truth, still less to fill any sphere of public or extended usefulness."[2]

We marvel that anyone could have judged Moody's future solely on his past and personal limitations. But unless seen in light of his eternal identity, a person is always reduced to a static, determined entity, a puppet manipulated by past and present influences. The temptation is to think, for instance, "Tom has had a volatile temper since he was a child. His father is hardly a paragon of self-control. Tom will never change."

The wonder of the gospel is God's power to restore His image in man. The most defeated and stumbling person among us can become, by God's grace, a radiant, confident overcomer. God calls us His bride, His temple, His field—all scriptural imagery that speaks of transformation. In Him, there is always hope.

What would our attitude be if we could see, with spiritual eyes, all that another person could be in Christ? "It is in the light of these overwhelming possibilities," C.S. Lewis said, "that we should conduct all our dealings with one another, all friendships, all loves, all play, all politics. There are no *ordinary* people. You have never talked to a mere mortal."[3] Looking beyond the limitations of our earthen vessels to the limitless potential *in Christ*, we see within us the hidden treasure of an eternal identity.

A willingness to be a model

When God wanted to communicate truth, He incarnated it. He Himself took the form of a man and lived before us, "and we beheld His glory, glory as of the only begotten from the Father, full of grace and truth" (John 1:14).

Words never seem to be enough. No matter how forcefully spoken or appropriately illustrated, they cannot compare with the powerful eloquence of a Christlike model, of a life that speaks volumes. Why else do we sit spellbound through the simple testimony of a believer who has walked with God through years of trial and triumph? His words have been purchased in the crucible of experience. The bone and marrow of his being embodies the truth he speaks. For the same reason we pore over

Christian biographies in search of a model, of a glimpse into lives that not only espouse but also *demonstrate* the truth.

One son explained the power of a Christlike life in this way: "In my rebellion against God I had contrived various means of discounting the Scripture and disproving the Resurrection. But what I could not dispute and what eventually brought me back to the Lord, was the reality of Jesus Christ in my Dad's life. That I could not deny."

In every age, God is seeking people through whom He can reveal Himself. He uses the lives of people, shaping them into living demonstrations of His grace and sufficiency. God cloaks Himself with our flesh.

How that model is formed

Eleanor had moved five times in the previous ten years, and when it came time to move again, she was gritting her teeth with the frustration of leaving and starting over—again. "I've lost the adventuresome spirit of my youth," she confessed to the Lord. "Finding new friends, new schools, and stepping over boxes just wasn't how I planned to spend this year."

Then she realized the paradox of what she was saying. If she really believed that what God accomplished *in* her life through the acceptance of difficult situations was more important than having life wrinkle-free, then she had to cooperate with the process. "Momentary, light affliction is producing for us an eternal weight of glory far beyond all comparison, while we look not at the things which are seen, but at the things which are not seen; for the things which are seen are temporal, but the things which are not seen are eternal" (2 Corinthians 4:17-18).

God pays us the "intolerable compliment" of loving us enough to make us like Christ in spite of whatever discomforts and trials that transformation might entail. Sometimes we would prefer to be left alone, but God has eternity in mind. "It is natural for us to wish that God had designed for us a less glorious and less arduous destiny; but then we are wishing not for more love but for less."[4]

A friend once described what had been the most influential factor in her development of a deep commitment to the Lord. She mentioned that her grandfather, who had lived with her family the last seven years of his life, had been her greatest source of motivation. "Those were very hard years for him," she said. "He was partially deaf, and he assumed God was, too. Night after night I'd stand outside his door, listening to him pray and read his Bible aloud. I could sense his utter dependence on God. As his physical life ebbed, his spiritual life was at its fullest. I could see God's grace in the midst of his difficulties, and I wanted the strength of character he had."

Because we are models of God's grace, He uses our difficulties not only to build our own character but also to influence the character of others. God "comforts us in all our affliction so that we may be able to comfort those who are in any affliction" with the same comfort God has given us (2 Corinthians 1:4). "There were never any prisons of suffering that I was in," the Quaker leader George Fox said, "but still it was for the bringing multitudes more out of prison."[5]

Spending ourselves for others

A frustrated psychiatrist once complained, "I can cure somebody's madness, but I can't do anything about that person's badness." He realized his inability to get to the root of the problem. Only the transforming power of God can change someone's nature. We, as His ambassadors, have the privilege of being part of that process of seeing Christ formed in someone else.

The gospel has a two-pronged effect: God reconciles us, and then He gives us the ministry of reconciling others to Himself. He asks us to invest our lives in other people as a logical response to recognizing their worth in His eyes, even as Jesus told Peter that if he really loved Him, he should feed His sheep (John 21:17).

There is nothing quite like the thrill of hearing a new Christian pray for the first time, or watching someone apply God's truth to a problem area of his life. It is the joy of a midwife after delivery, rejoicing in the movement and the shrill cry of new life.

To see people come to Christ or grow in Him is exciting. Even to help a person come just one step closer is no slight thing. As a young woman advising a college sorority, I was able to share the good news of Christ with so many girls that I could probably have drawn out the gospel illustration on a napkin in my sleep. Mostly I was met with the same ho-hum-I-need-to-get-back-to-my-homecoming-float response.

Once, after months of blank, bored faces, I talked with a girl who was convinced that all she needed was her confirmation certificate to be right with God. I shared a simple illustration with her about what it meant to trust Christ alone for her salvation. After listening quietly for a while, she looked up at me and said, "Yes, I see the difference. I see what you mean." It was as though I could see the Holy Spirit begin to part the veil in her mind. Although she didn't commit her life to Christ that day, the joy of seeing ripening fruit was so invigorating for me that it overshadowed an entire year of discouraging efforts.

The Apostle Paul wrote to the Thessalonian believers that they would be his crown of rejoicing when Christ returns (1 Thessalonians 2:19). This very same man who once had a consenting role in the stoning of Stephen now reveled in the inexpressible joy of seeing people come to believe in Jesus Christ.

This kind of joy does not come without personal cost. Paul spoke of extending to others not only the gospel but also his very life. In the process he experienced "conflicts without, fears within" (2 Corinthians 7:5). He knew what it was to be hungry, thirsty, poorly clothed, and homeless. He told his fellow believers that he would "most gladly spend and be expended for [their] souls" (2 Corinthians 12:15).

But what does this mean to the majority of us—

we who have little reason to fear being stoned or thrown out of town? It means that the investment of our lives in other people should be reflected in our values and in the choices we make. It means that people take precedence over things.

Since people are so important—eternally important—we should value their companionship in our home more than we should value the lovely dishes we use to serve them our most impressive meals. Having the time available to pursue relationships with nonChristians ought to be more attractive to us than climbing the corporate ladder on a sixty-hour week. We might need to make the decision to take a new Christian to a conference rather than running in the city marathon scheduled the same weekend. Or our commitment to people might mean choosing a deeper relationship with our children over a second income and a newer car.

Everyday life is a series of value judgments in which, when all the factors are weighed, the people-oriented factors should take priority. All our fondest projects, the unfinished do-lists, all the paraphernalia of modern life, we will leave behind in death. *People* are the stuff of eternity. A deep realization of this fact cannot help but affect how we spend our lives—today and forever.

Notes

1. Elisabeth Elliot, *Passion and Purity* (Old Tappan: Fleming H. Revell, 1984), page 185.
2. Stanley and Patricia Gundry, eds., *The Wit and Wis-*

dom of D.L. Moody (Grand Rapids: Baker, 1974), page 10.
3. C.S. Lewis, *The Weight of Glory* (Grand Rapids: Eerdmans, 1949), page 15.
4. C.S. Lewis, *The Problem of Pain*, page 31.
5. Amy Carmichael, *Gold by Moonlight* (Fort Washington: Christian Literature Crusade, 1935), page 33.

4
The Impact of One Life

> Without sacrifice there is no resurrection. Nothing grows and blooms save by giving. All you try to save in yourself wastes and perishes.
>
> *André Gide*

On the brink of the twenty-first century, we find ourselves swallowed up in a universe of baffling immensity and intricate variety. Long ago man mapped the heavens into neat patterns of constellations, but now he grapples with the knowledge of a hundred billion galaxies, each containing perhaps a hundred billion individual stars. With the psalmist, we pause to ask the question, "When I consider Thy heavens, the work of Thy fingers . . . What is man, that Thou dost take thought of him?" (Psalm 8:3-4). The larger the world seems, the more we question what makes our individual lives significant.

In answering that profound riddle, our generation has become preoccupied with discovering *self*—"as though it were something to be looked for, like a winning number in a lottery; then once found, to be hoarded and treasured."[1] Like children dancing around a flagpole until we're thoroughly dizzy, we have explored, analyzed, and encountered self from every possible angle, only to emerge dazed and groping. Our riddle is no closer to being solved.

In fact, with each new achievement we only dig ourselves deeper into a knotty morass of unanswered questions. The answers do not lie in ourselves. As Aleksandr Solzhenitsyn said, there is nowhere to look but up:

> If the world has not approached its end, it has reached a major watershed in history, equal in importance to the turn from the Middle Ages to the Renaissance. It will demand from us a spiritual blaze; we shall have to rise to a new height of vision, to a new level of life. . . . This ascension is similar to climbing onto the next anthropological stage. No one on earth has any other way left but—upward.

Only God provides the answer to the ancient riddle of the individual and the many, how the parts relate to the whole. Isaiah said of God's identity, "Your Redeemer is the Holy One of Israel, who is called the God of all the earth" (Isaiah 54:5). He is God of the infinite and of the particular. The microcosm of my life takes on meaning only as it is related to the macrocosm of all God's eternal purposes.

God and the individual

There is a recurring theme in Scripture about how the obscure, the weak, the ordinary, the *individual*, can have a profound effect on the whole. The Bible is a collection of individuals used by God to accomplish His expansive purposes in history. He seems to delight in affecting the many through the few.

How can we comprehend the mystery that God would use fallen and frail individuals to reveal His eternal truths? We detect throughout Scripture that the great men and women of faith were ordinary people with more than ordinary weaknesses. Yet God accomplished eternally significant things through their lives.

During one of Israel's lowest points in history, their enemies, the Midianites, were destroying their produce and livestock, and devastating their land. All of Israel was cowering in fear and dread. The angel of the Lord singled out one man, Gideon, to deliver God's people—a man who was the youngest member of the weakest family of his tribe.

When the angel appeared to Gideon, he addressed him with these amazing words: "The LORD is with you, O valiant warrior" (Judges 6:12). You can almost see Gideon looking over his shoulder to see who on earth this angel was talking to. Gideon then proceeded to protest that God had apparently abandoned Israel and that he was certainly no candidate to deliver the nation. When Gideon finally chose to follow the angel's instructions, he did so at night for fear of reprisal, and then, only after God had proved Himself by a miraculous sign. Valiant warrior, indeed!

Yet Gideon, with God's help, led a band of three hundred men to victory over a host of enemy soldiers, who were "as numerous as locusts" (Judges 7:12). God, we must always remember, is not bound by man's limitations in accomplishing His purposes.

Not only does God use ordinary people, but He also requires that they obey *in faith*, without seeing the full fruits of their obedience. Look at the witness of Abraham or Joseph or Hannah, and try for a moment to divest them of their Sunday-school, larger-than-life aura. Let them be ordinary pedestrians of their day, shuffling hot sand between their toes.

Who could have guessed that one man and his entourage ambling through the desert would become the family through whom all the people on earth would be blessed? Or that a teenager, double-crossed by his rival siblings, could provide by his forgiveness and God's promotion the land where the chosen people would flourish and multiply?

Or consider a distraught Hannah in the temple, praying for a child so fervently that she appeared drunk. Think how she felt taking her only child—who was the answer to her many prayers—to live with a weak, indulgent old man, to be without the benefit of nursery school, swimming lessons, and (most of all) *her*. Hannah could not have known at that point that God would give her five more children and that the one she "gave away" would become perhaps the most godly, influential judge of Israel's history. What an incredible impact one life can make!

Abraham, Joseph, and Hannah did not see the outcome of their obedience. God promised Abraham that He would multiply his descendants as the stars of the heavens and the sand of the seashore. Yet how much fulfillment of that promise did Abraham live to see? Only Isaac, Ishmael, and the sons of a few concubines.

For these biblical characters—Abraham, Joseph, and Hannah—the pipeline of the future was as closed off as it is to us. They had to believe by faith that God had a plan for and through their lives—a plan that was worth the struggle of wandering around in the desert or shivering in a dingy prison cell or renouncing motherhood's claim upon a long-awaited child.

And even now . . .

The challenge before us is to learn from these biblical examples, realizing that the individual is still God's key to the whole world. He lays His hand upon the foolish, the weak, the base, and the despised to accomplish His purposes (1 Corinthians 1:26-29). He specializes in transforming those who could not into those who can.

Aleksandr Solzhenitsyn, Nobel prize winner and veteran of Soviet work camps, tells of a young Jewish doctor named Boris Kornfield, who shared his newfound faith in Christ with him in a frigid Siberian prison. As Solzhenitsyn lay recovering from cancer surgery, Boris spent a few hours one night at his bedside telling the story of his spiritual journey.

Boris ended his story that night with these words, which were some of his very last: "On the whole . . . I have become convinced that there is no punishment that comes to us in this life on earth which is undeserved. . . . If you go over your life with a fine-tooth comb and ponder it deeply, you will always be able to hunt down that transgression of yours for which you received this blow." Boris never lived to see the response of his patient. His head was smashed in that very night by some men who were angry that he was fighting against the Soviet system. His words lay upon Solzhenitsyn as an inheritance he could not readily shrug off.

Solzhenitsyn lay wide awake many sleepless nights, pondering his life and the unexpected turns it had taken. "Gradually it was disclosed to me," he said, "that the line separating good and evil passes not through states, not between classes, nor between political parties either—but right through every human heart." The man at last came face to face with the evil in his own heart. He set down his transformed thoughts in verse:

> And now with measuring cup returned to me,
> Scooping up the living water,
> God of the Universe! I believe again!
> Though I renounced You, You were with me![2]

The name of Boris Kornfield will probably not be entered in the annals of history. Certainly according to the world's terms, he was a failure. But if it had not been for this relatively unknown man in a remote Siberian prison, one of the greatest thinkers and spokesmen of our century—Aleksandr Solzhenitsyn—might not have found the path to life in Christ.

John Haggai, a writer and evangelist to the third world, tells the story of an individual—his son—whose life had profound influence far beyond himself. Because his son Johnny was delivered by a thoroughly drunk obstetrician, the boy lived twenty-four years with severely crippling handicaps. Johnny was never able to utter more than two syllables: "yeah" for yes and "umn" for no. He could not dress himself or care for any of his own needs. His mother poured her life into him.

But inside the prison of Johnny's incapacitated body lived a lively, competent mind. As his father returned from trips overseas and described to him all that God was doing in the third world, Johnny developed a deep spiritual burden for those unreached people. He devoted himself to hours of prayer for world outreach and for his father's ministry with national evangelists. Only heaven will tell what victories in world evangelism were won through the years of sustained, faithful prayer by one whose existence the world would call a tragic mistake.[3]

But these are dramatic examples. Not many of us will lead a Solzhenitsyn to Christ. Only the unique circumstances of a few will open such vistas of intercessory prayer. Where does that leave the majority of us who take meals to lonely old people, or befriend an unbeliever at work, or pray over babies as we diaper them?

It leaves us in that same stream of history, believing by faith that God will use our self-sacrificing lives in a greater way than we could ever foresee. Isaiah said, "The smallest one will become a clan, and the least one a mighty nation. I, the LORD, will hasten it in its time" (Isaiah 60:22). God multiplies His life in people, but in His time.

We are not able, from our limited view, to count the ripples that result from our little pebbles in the pond. But our confidence is that God is at work in and through our lives. As D.L. Moody once said, "There is nothing small that God is in."[4] The slight glimpse of fruit that we see now will come into full view in eternity. We trust that we will eventually experience the joy of meeting people our physical and spiritual children have influenced for Christ.

God makes us members of His Body, His people. Our lives should take on the significance of being a vital part of that whole. There is no room in Christ's Body for boasting or jealous comparisons with others who appear to be making a bigger splash. Our efforts in the Body are inextricably intertwined. My significance is wrapped up in yours, and yours in mine.

But our worth and significance before God is not dependent on our accomplishments for His Kingdom. "The worth of the individual" is not just a utilitarian phrase that connects a person's spiritual significance with his usefulness to God, as though God were wringing His hands in need of our services. God will accomplish His purposes in history, with or without us. By His *grace* we are able to have a part, the extent of which only the future course of eternity will accurately reveal.

High privilege, high calling

We praise God's "glorious generosity" (Ephesians 1:6, PH), which redeemed us from a fruitless, meaningless existence and made us His ambassadors, the showpieces of His handiwork. This privilege, however, may negate some of our previous plans.

Before racial tensions reached their height in the 1960s, a young man named John Perkins left Mississippi with his wife and headed for a new life in California. He left behind him the poverty and rejection he'd grown up with. He tried to close his mind to the memories of white police officers who shot his favorite brother and went unpunished.

In California the doors opened to home ownership and a secure, advancing job. But the move to California took an even more significant turn that John had not counted on. One day John went with his son Spencer to church in order to appease him, and found himself a spiritual captive. "What drew me to Christ," John says, "is that for the first time I knew I was loved."[5]

As John grew spiritually, he began to minister in prisons. There he came to realize that the problems of the ghetto were the unsolved problems of the South. He sensed that God was calling him back to Mississippi—the last place he wanted to go.

But he went. He moved his family into Mendenhall, one of the poorest of black communities. There he combined evangelism and social action with such an overwhelmingly positive response that now, twenty-five years after, Mendenhall is the model for countless community efforts for Christ.

John did lose out in some ways on the untroubled, comfortable life his family could have enjoyed in the suburbs of California. But God gave him instead an extraordinary impact on people. As he now sees whole communities changed for Christ, doubtless the loss of a "comfortable" life seems a small price.

For any of us, there is a price to pay if we would invest our lives in God's eternal purposes. But if we turn inward and become self-oriented as our culture has, our lives will have no more lasting significance than the lives of the Epicureans. These ancient Greek lovers of pleasure vowed to eat, drink, and be merry, for they saw nothing in the future or the past that had any profound bearing on the present.

In order to find significance, I must lose my life in something greater than myself. C.S. Lewis explains well the ultimate solution to man's quest for true identity:

> Our whole destiny seems to lie . . . in acquiring a fragrance that is not our own but borrowed, in becoming clean mirrors filled with the image of a face that is not ours. . . . I am not, in my natural state, nearly so much of a person as I like to believe. . . . It is when I turn to Christ, when I

> give myself up to His Personality, that I first begin to have a real personality of my own.[6]

In a magazine advertisement for a humane society, there is a photograph of a dog and a cat sitting side by side in uncustomary harmony. The caption over their heads is, "A Couple of VIP's—Very Important Pets." And in the fine print underneath, the next line adds, "What makes them important is who owns them."

That same fine-print legend could be written under our pictures. What makes us important is who owns us. What gives our lives significance is having a part in His plan. May we be like David, who "served the purpose of God in his own generation" (Acts 13:36).

Notes

1. Malcolm Muggeridge, *Something Beautiful for God* (New York: Harper & Row, 1971), page 17.
2. Aleksandr Solzhenitsyn, *The Gulag Archipelago, II* (New York: Harper & Row, 1975), pages 613-615.
3. John Haggai, *My Son Johnny* (Wheaton: Tyndale, 1978).
4. Stanley and Patricia Gundry, eds., *D. L. Moody,* page 72.
5. Interview with John Perkins, conducted by Paula Rinehart in May 1985.
6. C.S. Lewis, "Christianity and Literature," *Christian Reflections,* Walter Hooper, ed. (Grand Rapids: Eerdmans, 1967), page 7; C.S. Lewis, *Mere Christianity,* page 189.

5 Ambition: Vice or Virtue?

The figure of the Crucified invalidates all thought that takes success for its standard.

Dietrich Bonhoeffer

When Nikita Khrushchev was in power in the Soviet Union, he managed to antagonize many of his comrades. He angered the KGB by publicly denouncing Stalin's crimes. He alarmed bureaucrats by imposing new rules on party organization. His gamble in Cuba ended in utter disgrace.

All of these blunders, however, would have been excused as merely intemperate but pardonable decisions made by a man laboring over a bloated bureaucracy. But the final and intolerable blow came when he encroached upon the holy of holies, the inner sanctum of the ruling class. His downfall was assured when he challenged the position and power of ambitious party men.

Tom Wolfe analyzes the ambition of fighter-pilots-turned-astronauts in his humorous exposé, *The Right Stuff.* Here were men with monstrous egos, he said, who were climbing an invisible ladder to prove they had the right stuff to be astronauts. What motivated them was largely the fear of being left behind in the race.

Worldly ambition can by no means be limited to the halls of the Kremlin or the hangars of fighter pilots. Each of us, to some degree, recognizes within a desire not merely to do well but to be *first,* to be among the inner circle. "I believe," C.S. Lewis said, "that in all men's lives at certain periods . . . one of the most dominant elements is the desire to be inside the local Ring and the terror of being left outside."[1]

Such a drive is unfortunately no stranger to me. Before I came to Christ, I enlisted in the U.S. Army for Officer Candidate School, trying to avoid being drafted as a lowly private. So I was on my way to becoming Lieutenant Stacy Rinehart. In OCS, we were required to wear a black fiberglass helmet, inside which we were to pin a brass second lieutenant's bar to fan the flames of aspiration. But I couldn't stop with just one bar. Intoxicated by the hope of that upward climb, I added insignias for first lieutenant, captain, major, and every other rank all the way up to a four-star general. Inside my helmet the whole upper echelon of the army was represented. Needless to say, it weighed much more than the helmets of my companions—in many ways.

After I became a Christian, my ambitious drive to achieve seemed so woefully inconsistent with faith in One who spoke worlds into existence and yet allowed Himself to be hung on a cross between two thieves. And as I began to read the Bible, I was dismayed to see examples of people who had only thinly veiled their ambitious drive behind the cloak of religious pretense. I was forced to grapple with the question, Is ambition necessarily a vice or can it be a virtue?

When I turned to the account of the Israelites *en route* to the Promised Land, there were Miriam and Aaron bickering over who should have the privilege of speaking for God. "Has the LORD indeed spoken only through Moses? Has He not spoken through us as well?" (Numbers 12:2). Miriam and Aaron were voicing a timeless question, one that presupposes spiritual leadership as a means to corner and administer the power of God.

The New Testament contains even more blatant examples than the Old. A close look at the Pharisees reveals men distraught over far more than the miracles and message of a Righteous Man. "If we let Him go on like this," they said, ". . . the Romans will come and take away both our place and our nation" (John 11:48). The threat of lost position was even greater than their distaste for Christ's theology.

Even among the disciples, those closest to Jesus, there was a strange preoccupation with status in their Master's future Kingdom. During the Last Supper, there was a dispute among them over who would be the greatest in that Kingdom. As you read this account in Scripture, you can almost see the disciples elbowing each other for the choicest seats at the table (Luke 22:14-24).

Thus, in both the secular and the religious realms, it would seem that ambition is imbedded in a person's makeup. The drive to subdue and have dominion over the earth is part of the nature of man. Somehow, though, this sense of purpose, this God-given drive, becomes twisted into egocentricity. We serve our own ends and, worse yet, we sometimes do so in religious guise.

God wants to take what is essentially the perversion of a virtue and redirect it toward righteous ends. The truth of that revelation came as no small encouragement to me, the second-lieutenant-going-on-general. For I was often guilty of caricaturing spiritual Christians as rather bland, innocuous people who use God to sanction their mediocrity.

It was strangely comforting to realize that Christ does not choose as His followers those who have nothing else to do, those who are in a corner just watching the parade of life go by. When Jesus met Simon the zealot, Simon was a man fully bent on overthrowing Rome; Matthew was determined to get rich by any means; Peter and Andrew were entrepreneurs of a small but successful fishing venture. The disciples were heading in a questionable direction in some cases—but at least they were heading somewhere.

Eighteenth-century statesman and reformer William Wilberforce said, "Christianity proposes not to extinguish our natural desires. It promises to bring the desires under just control and direct them to their true object."[2] When we set out on a path of following Christ, He begins work in the deeper recesses of the personality to change our self-centered ambitions into godly ones with lasting, eternal value.

Pleasing God

On one of the few occasions in which the Apostle Paul ever spoke of his ambitions, he said, "We have as our ambition . . . to be pleasing to Him" (2 Corinthians 5:9). Paul was instructing the Corinthians to do whatever they did for the Lord.

To speak of doing something in order to please God, to be driven by that kind of motivation, can seem strange, like a grade school child who diligently works on his memory verse so that he can get a check on his Sunday school chart. But what Paul speaks of here is very different. He is saying that when God saved us, something of cosmic significance took place. We were transferred from the dominion of darkness to the Kingdom of His Son. The debt we owed was paid in full.

That's why the writer of Hebrews said, "Since we receive a kingdom which cannot be shaken, let us show gratitude, by which we may offer to God an acceptable service" (Hebrews 12:28). If we have an appreciation of what God has done for us, the only rational response we can have is to long for a life that pleases Him. No other motivation or drive will sustain us when the going gets tough.

Paul goes on to add, "For we must all appear before the judgment-seat of Christ, that each one may be recompensed for his deeds . . . whether good or bad" (2 Corinthians 5:10). Paul never lost sight of the reality of standing before Christ, of seeing his life evaluated by a Higher Authority. The hope of hearing "Well done, thou good and faithful servant" (Matthew 25:21, KJV) would make any earthly employer's promotion or pat on the back seem trifling by comparison. This desire to please the Lord, to be welcomed by His favoring countenance, is no second-rate motivation. It is a primary human drive.

Experiencing an eternal sense of purpose
Deep within our consciousness is the drive to know what we were made for, the sense that God has something particular in mind for each of our lives. Paul considered his early social, religious, and educational achievements insignificant compared with knowing Christ. What drove him forward in the Christian life? The desire to know more of Christ and to "lay hold of that for which also [he] was laid hold of" (Philippians 3:12).

The Old Testament account of Joseph is a rags-to-riches story we love to recount. Yet even when he was in the rags phase in prison, Joseph was sustained by the same thing that kept him going when he was at the right hand of Pharaoh's throne: a sense that God had an eternal purpose for his life of much greater importance than his own personal comfort.

Thus Joseph could assure his brothers that God had used the repercussions of their evil betrayal for His purposes, "to preserve many people alive" (Genesis 50:20). Each of us needs to be able to say, "I am here because God has put me here, because He intends to bring something from my life in this place."

This progress took a while for a businessman named Dutch Karickhoff, but eventually God got hold of his life. Dutch was a nominal Christian completely consumed with his insurance business and various civic activities. He and his wife were communicating very little at the time.

Much to his surprise, his city gave him the coveted Serviceman of the Year Award. That evening his friends took him out to celebrate. The local newspapers called his wife to interview her, but she knew nothing about it. When Dutch returned that night, there was a large note on the door: "Who in the ____ are you now?"

For days that question reverberated in his mind. "God let me achieve everything I sought," he said, "and then showed me how empty it was." He began to sense that God had some purpose for his life beyond stacking up awards, some purpose he had been oblivious to.

This question about his identity began the transformation of Dutch's life and ambition. He subsequently began to commit to God any aspect of his life that God brought to mind. "I used to drive around the block where my business was located, for instance, and offer that business back to God. 'Here, Lord, You can have this. It's Yours.' After a few months, I sensed that the business no longer owned me."

Dutch is still in the insurance business, but

he is there for different reasons and with a different purpose. The years that followed have brought him countless opportunities in his professional and private life to touch people for Christ.[3]

Redefining success

Western culture is a skillful teacher, carefully and persistently indoctrinating her children, forming in their minds a model for success and achievement. A spacious home, smart and attractive children, job recognition, athletic prowess—everywhere we turn we are reminded what to strive for.

Somehow, though, when we begin to grasp eternal values, all that this world holds as standards of success seems flat, like soda pop without the fizz. We begin asking healthy questions. "What difference does it all make? Is this all there is to life?"

Our growth in the Lord is an illuminating pilgrimage in which God substitutes another vision and another set of ambitions for the ones we've been taught so well. Like a sailor who climbs to the lookout at the top of the mast, we glimpse from our new vantage a Kingdom that cannot be shaken, one with a different set of scales for measuring achievement. Our focus becomes the purpose of the King, a noble spiritual task rather than mere position, wealth, or personal recognition.

But is it possible, I am often asked, to follow God wholeheartedly and still achieve something according to this world's terms? Are the two antithetical? If we allow God to rechannel our ambitions so that they reflect eternal values, are we doomed to the back alleys of worldly achievement?

In the Old Testament we read of at least a few examples of godly men who were successful by worldly standards: "The LORD was with Joseph, so he became a successful man" (Genesis 39:2). Joseph enjoyed all the position, power, and wealth we commonly associate with successful people. Prison had purified him so that he saw his good fortune for what it was: position and wealth loaned to him for a time and a purpose.

God may indeed grant worldly success to spiritual people. He refuses to be pigeonholed, however. He offers no guarantees. When Job's wealth and family were destroyed, he said, "The LORD gave and the LORD has taken away. Blessed be the name of the LORD" (Job 1:21). Job could release his earthly treasures to the Lord in the midst of calamity because his hand had not clung to them in prosperity.

To spiritual people, worldly success is usually of minor consequence. It happens *incidentally,* without great premeditated calculation. The common components of modern success—position, power, and wealth—are factors that God could either add to or subtract from our lives. It should make little difference to us one way or the other.

Seeing God transform our ambitions

The foundational question to be dealt with is one of motives: What drives me to do what I do? Am I imprisoned by images of how I would have defined success in my past? Have I reconsidered the validity of these images now that I know Christ?

A purely surface examination of our lives—what Bible studies we attend, our involvement at church—will not suffice. We must allow God to change the whole structure of how we value ourselves and what we consider important. Otherwise we will be forever chasing the elusive phantoms of larger homes or job promotions—to which we merely tack on religious activity.

The real spiritual quality of our ambition is determined by our *motives,* which are by nature hard to measure and perpetually mixed. In considering those, we have to periodically ask ourselves some hard questions: Do I continue even when the results of my efforts are meager, the praise slight? Do I find myself fondling dreams of grandeur, what the Bible calls the vain imaginings of position, recognition, and wealth? Must I always have my name attached to my efforts or achievements? Must I receive personal recognition in order to continue? Could I walk off and leave what I'm doing at any time if I was convinced God wanted me to? Do I feel I need the position of some achievement to give me a platform to share Christ effectively, or am I willing to be a witness as an ordinary person who depends on God's power to make him extraordinary?

These questions can lead you into the necessary cleansing process of reassessing your ambitions in life. Sometimes that reassessment leads to renouncing previous motivations and goals. This means starting mentally again with a clean slate and allowing God to give back what He pleases—

only purified. A friend of ours, a skillful engineer, moved to Texas in order to get spiritual training and expertise in helping others grow. He lived for a year just barely making ends meet by flying for the Air Force Reserves. The humility of being without a "real" job cast its shadow on that time. But later on he realized that during that process, God was extracting many of the impurities from his former ambition and love of engineering. Eventually he returned to his career field, but engineering was no longer an obsession.

A helpful passage for such experiences in our lives is this: "In the wilderness He fed you manna which your fathers did not know, that He might humble you and that He might test you, to do good for you in the end. Otherwise, you may say in your heart, 'My power and the strength of my hand made me this wealth'" (Deuteronomy 8:16-17). God takes His children by a different route than we would choose on our own. He allows the humbling mortification of our self-assurance, lest we be swallowed up in the future by the pride of "our" achievement.

God knows us too well. He knows man's propensity for attributing his achievements to his own ingenuity and effort, much like Nebuchadnezzar, the king who strolled his palace rooftop overlooking Babylon, saying, "Is this not Babylon the great, which I myself have built . . . by the might of my power and for the glory of my majesty?" (Daniel 4:30). Even as the words were still coming from his mouth, God reduced him to a wild wanderer, more animal than man. Eventually, when he came to his sanity and his senses, this wandering king on earth praised the King of Heaven, the God that Nebuchadnezzar, in the blindness of his pride, had forgotten.

Those who have walked with God for years through the wilderness experiences of life usually exhibit an imperturbable disinterest in power and position. Moses entreated the Lord to remove the plague from his sister, Miriam, a plague she had acquired by usurping *his* authority and position. In his youth, David refused to raise his hand against Saul, who was God's anointed authority. He would become king only when God so chose to make him king. In his old age, he refused to maneuver to remain Israel's king, even to preserve his kingdom against the attacks of his own son.

For most of us, ambition is a strong inner drive waiting to overpower us. But God wants to take that drive and redirect it toward righteous ends. He wants to refashion our inner motivations.

God is not content with just the spillover or the surplus of our lives. He wants to reach into the core of our personal identity, placing His claim upon it. Only when we allow Him full entrance there will we find ourselves on a course that will honor Him.

Notes

1. C.S. Lewis, *The Weight of Glory*, page 58.
2. William Wilberforce, *Real Christianity* (Portland: Multnomah, 1982), page 65.
3. Interview with Dutch Karickhoff, conducted by Paula Rinehart.

6
The Significance of Work

It is inbred in us that we have to do exceptional things for God, but we have not. We have to be exceptional in the ordinary things, to be holy in mean streets and among mean people.

Oswald Chambers

The speaker paused for just a moment and reached for the glass of water beside the podium. What a privilege to address this group of Christians, he thought. These men and women represent Jesus Christ on a daily basis in law offices and libraries, in classrooms and department stores, in laboratories and factories.

He continued with his talk. "Your clients and customers, as well as the people you work with, may never darken the doorstep of your church. Thus the question you must ask is this: Does the aroma of Christ emanate from your life? How would the spiritual atmosphere change if you suddenly left your position at work? Would you, today, be willing to commit yourself to serving

Christ where you are, in your respective arena of influence at work?"

Before he could go any further, a young professional uninhibitedly raised his hand. "I would love to serve Christ as you suggest," he said, "but I work eight hours a day."

Have you ever felt like that? Has it seemed to you that serving Christ and holding down a full-time job were unevenly matched in a daily tug of war? The typical eight-to-five routine seems like a black hole of meaninglessness in the average Christian's life. A question we routinely struggle with is this: How can we fashion this maze of budgets to be balanced, letters to be typed, and papers to be graded into anything at all of spiritual shape or importance?

Whether we dread each day of work or savor every hour, the average person spends fifty to sixty percent of his waking hours on the job. We long to feel that our presence at work, day in and day out, makes some eternal difference.

To begin with, Scripture presents a paradoxical message about work. Adam was given the responsible position of tending the Garden. Yet after the Fall, much of the pleasure of his work was taken away by nonproductivity and frustration. We see in Ecclesiastes that Solomon struggled with the meaning of life in general and of work in particular. On the one hand, Solomon saw man's work as God's gift, and a good gift at that; on the other hand, he abhorred the thought of leaving the fruit of his labor to some fool in the future.

On the subject of work, as always, the Bible is

frightfully honest. Ever since the Fall, work has become an ambivalent mixture of bane and blessing, curse and gift. Man has struggled ever since to overcome the unpleasantness and to reinstate in work something of the holiness and pleasure of the Garden.

God Himself discloses His nature by the work He performs. In spite of the Fall, the fundamental element of work gains dignity from His example. Carl Henry speaks of God as "the Great Worker" who created order from chaos. "He stands by his work; he does not abandon it. There is no 'moral holiday,' no unjustifiable strike, no premature retirement."[1]

We may take this thought for granted, but to the Greek-thinking world into which the gospel came, this was a revolutionary idea. To the Greeks, God might be a great Thinker, but surely not a Worker—He could not soil His hands with the earthy process of Creation.

Christianity, in contrast, is a movement unembarrassed that its first disciples included a fisherman and a tax-gatherer, and whose greatest apostle was a tent maker. David, the great Old Testament king, began life without apology as a shepherd. And had not Christ Himself been a carpenter?

Christianity alone etches a true halo around man's daily labor, illuminating it as a means of glorifying God and benefiting society. This is an amazing thought in view of the fact that the earth and its works, including the buildings we design and the cabinets we carve, will be consumed in the intense heat of "the day of the Lord" (2 Peter 3:10). Of what value to God is the work of our hands, then? And if it has no value, why work?

Think for a moment of the carefully scribbled picture your kindergartner brings you. Only God and your child know what all those splotches of color mean. But you receive that picture with the joy of a parent and put it on your refrigerator door because you know full well the *true* market value of such art.[2]

Just so, God assigns value to the work of your hands. Knowing the final destination of the product of your efforts, knowing that man ultimately can add nothing to His own work, God, in His grace, imputes worth to your work out of His love relationship with you as His child. Although the product of our work will perish in the flames, the substance of our labor takes on *eternal* significance when performed as an offering to God, a platform for ministry, and a service to others.

An offering to God

Aleksandr Solzhenitsyn spent ten years of his life doing slave labor in a Soviet work camp. Though he performed harsh physical labor under abhorrent conditions, he was amazed to observe that "such is man's nature that even bitter, detested work is sometimes performed with an incomprehensible wild excitement."[3] Solzhenitsyn would find himself at times, for no apparent reason, totally engrossed in laying bricks precisely where they ought to be, as though he were creating a work of art.

We have all experienced brief flashes of unexplainable excitement in our work. But what will sustain our motivation over the long haul? As a man of broad interests, I have personally sampled quite a few jobs in the smorgasbord of work opportunities—everything from carpentry, painting, and managing a sixty-person work force in the fast food industry to ten years of leading discipling ministries. In every case, there have been certain periods of monotony and tedious routine. To look for "fulfillment" from any job is expecting more from work than God ever intended.

The only thing that will transform our work into the sacramental endeavor God intended, sustaining our inner motivation, is to offer that work to the Lord. "Here, Lord. I perform this task for Your sake, simply because You are worthy of my best effort." As Paul said, "It is the Lord Christ whom you serve" (Colossians 3:24).

But we cannot effectively offer up to God something that we quietly doubt His interest in. "Perhaps," we reason, "God is more pleased with my prayers and remodeling efforts on the church sanctuary than in the computers I program." And although we insist that this is not the case, our attitudes usually tell a different story. Unless we grasp in a deep, personal way that any work done "unto the Lord" is the work of the Lord, we will relegate the teeth we straighten or the diapers we change to a graveyard of secondary concerns.

Brother Lawrence, a sixteenth-century Carmelite monk who spent much of his years in the monastery's kitchen as a cook, described how he learned to practice the presence of God by offering his work to the Lord as an ongoing act of love and obedience.

> I turn my little omelette in the pan for the love of God. . . . When I can do nothing else, it is enough to have picked up a straw for the love of God. People look for ways of learning how to love God. . . . They take much trouble to abide in His presence by varied means. Is it not a shorter and more direct way to do everything for the love of God, to make use of all the tasks one's lot in life demands to show Him that love? . . . There is nothing complicated about it. One has only to turn to it honestly and simply.[4]

What is especially instructive about Brother Lawrence's example is that his experience of God came not through extensive contemplative reading or self-abasement but in the midst of his *work*, the simple but physically demanding work of preparing food.

If holiness is what we long for, there is perhaps no better training ground than work. A difficult boss, feelings of failure and inadequacy, and the high-pressure demands of the job can all be used by God as refining agents, forcing us to deal with flaws in our character that may never surface except under pressure. We don't need to enter a monastery or go to other unusual extremes in order to experience God. As we offer our work to Him, this work in itself can become a means of knowing Him.

A platform for ministry

When an architect designs a great building, his name is etched as a commemoration in a bronze plaque upon the side. A movie almost always ends with stirring music and a list of credit lines honoring its designers. Yet somehow man has managed to rob the Author of the universe of the glory and honor due Him, attributing His masterworks to evolution, chance, and even man himself. But we can do something about this negligence. The work that we perform provides the opportunity to bring honor to the One to whom it is due.

Samuel Johnson, the father of modern lexicography, labored for nine years to compile the first comprehensive dictionary, one that formed the crest of English literature for the eighteenth century. What motivated him in his daily meticulous search for the derivation and meaning of scarcely used words? Within the first few pages of his dictionary, he revealed the explanation for his compulsion for excellence in his work. He explained that this effort was "dedicated to the glory of God." His work was an extension of his life with God, work that brought either credit or dishonor to the Lord.

If we could actually engrave "dedicated to the glory of God" on the television set we repair or the music lesson we teach, then perhaps we would be more forcibly reminded that our work is a testimony to His work in us.

Our jobs provide the most visible platform available to demonstrate to people around us that God is real. We are, as Paul said, "a spectacle to the world" (1 Corinthians 4:9). Amy Carmichael, missionary to India's abandoned temple children, discovered quickly that the work there required many doctors, nurses, builders, craftsmen, and cooks—but there could be none who were *only* preachers. As a bewildered Hindu once said, "We have heard your preaching, but could you show us some of the *life* of this Lord Jesus?"

It is in the daily work we perform that we are best able to reveal the Life behind the sermon. We represent Christ, or as Martin Luther liked to say, "God milks the cows through you." We have ample opportunity to demonstrate a credible faith in our response to the pressures of life, the needs of people, and the temptation to shade the truth. One Christian employed in a large corporate structure said that he prays daily for God to make him like Nehemiah: a man ready with a righteous answer for an opportune moment.

But before a person is prepared to view his job as a platform for ministry, he must wrestle through the same tough questions anyone who enters vocational Christian work has to deal with. For a pastor to accept a position of service mainly because it offers attractive retirement benefits or a larger salary or the opportunity for promotion would be a breach of commitment and integrity, and rightly so. Is it significantly different for the layman? Are there special laymen's escape clauses written into the uncompromising biblical demands for following Jesus? If, indeed, the layman is also called to follow his Lord on a fulltime basis—not taking daily breaks from being a Christian—then it is no more acceptable for him than for any Christian worker to determine his course of action primarily on the basis of lucrative benefits or attractive job titles.

Each of us has a particular niche from which to serve God. The appropriate area of service for any Christian is determined by our *gifts* and our *calling*, by having prostrated ourselves before a real and personal God who will hold us accountable, asking Him, "Lord, what do *You* want me to do with my life? Where can You best use me?" The vast majority of His children He plants as undercover agents in "secular" jobs. He directs us, as He did His disciples, to let down our nets and to allow Him to fill them. But at any point He might also turn right around, as Jesus did with Peter and Andrew, and ask us to leave our nets in the sand and move on.

There are so many alternatives if we are willing to think creatively and strategically. Most of us could easily free up financial resources by cutting back on our lifestyle. Many of us have negotiable hours we waste in meaningless activities—hours that could be invested in spiritually profitable ways. A few of us have the option of living adequately on three or four days' salary instead of five, thereby freeing up extra hours to serve God in another capacity.

Only the layman who is convinced that God, not his company or business, will provide his material needs is truly free to serve God in his job. Those lyrical verses in the Sermon on the Mount about lilies of the field and birds of the air were not written exclusively to pastors and missionaries. The so-called layman, if left to his own ingenuity to provide for his needs, is left in a position where all he can do is be a slave to the company. For such a person, the willingness to take risks, to take a stand as a Christian, to bear with an incapacitated employee, gradually evaporates in the quiet but paralyzing fear of losing income.

But answering the question, "Am I where God wants me?" is only half the consideration. We must also address the question, "Am I doing what God wants in the place where He has put me?"

One friend of ours, a seasoned veteran of personal Bible study, worked as a journalist for a large metropolitan newspaper. She was once asked to do a special Sunday section on women, spotlighting the various roles and achievements of local women. When we read her section, we looked in vain for just one example of a woman who had chosen the unfashionable role of homemaker and mother, for just one woman who mentioned her family as a significant priority. There was none.

When we asked our friend why she had interviewed only upwardly-mobile career women, she expressed genuine surprise. As we talked, she began to reconsider the strategic position God had placed her in. Because she realized the biblical worth of homemaking and mothering, she should have given some mention of the role of wife and mother in the article. In failing to do so, she was forfeiting the platform God had given her in her job.

Scripture cannot be restricted to the personal sanctum of our lives, applied only in the private confines of our devotional habits and family relationships. If we want our work to genuinely demonstrate the reality of God, we must integrate what we know spiritually into the public world of work and business.

Service to others

The concept of work that is valued because it benefits *people* is all but lost in the modern marketplace. Work nowadays is largely seen as a commodity we exchange for the fruits of consumption.

To the Puritans, from whom we in Western society largely derive our work ethic, a godly man worked not so much to accumulate as to add to the comfort and convenience of the community. He fulfilled his vocation the best he could, and whatever resultant degree of wealth and prominence God brought was purely secondary.

Christ gave the basis for viewing work as a service to others. He stated that to whatever extent we meet someone else's needs, we do that for Him. "To the extent that you did it to one of these brothers of Mine, even the least of them, you did it to Me" (Matthew 25:40).

By some unseen transferral system, the labor we do, even the simple cup of water we offer, is done not just for the person across the counter but for Him. In our world, even with people who are healthy and attractive and especially with people who are suffering and dying, we must frequently remind ourselves that the very image of God is imprinted on the people we serve. Yet there is probably nothing that reveals more clearly Christ's presence in us than our sensitivity and regard for people.

Unless our secular jobs become sacred work, unless His aroma is allowed to permeate the marketplace through us, our labor will echo the daily grind of a perpetual treadmill, an ongoing waste of time. If I am not serving Christ in the physically and emotionally demanding aspects of my life that I call "work," then I am not fully serving Christ.

God offers us something more. We love to quote Paul's words: "Be steadfast, immovable, always abounding in the work of the Lord, knowing that your toil is not in vain in the Lord" (1 Corinthians 15:58). This encouraging promise follows immediately after Paul's explanation of how this body of fragile flesh will one day take on immortality. In some mysterious way, the Lord will transform a body that is earthy, ordinary, and subject to decay into one that is imperishable—in short, eternal.

God has promised a similar metamorphosis in our work. Work that is performed as an offering to Him, as though He Himself were present in those we serve, will not have been "in vain," either in this life or in the one to come.

Notes

1. Carl Henry, *Aspects of Christian Social Ethics* (Grand Rapids: Baker Book House, 1981), page 51.
2. We are indebted to Walt Henrichsen and his fine

tape, "Why Go to Work?" for this insight and analogy.

3. Aleksandr Solzhenitsyn, *The Gulag Archipelago, II*, page 259.
4. Brother Lawrence, *The Practice of the Presence of God* (Nashville: Thomas Nelson, 1982), page 85.

7
Living with Purpose

> We always pay dearly for chasing after what is cheap.
>
> *Aleksandr Solzhenitsyn*

In 1850, Feodor Dostoevsky, the literary giant of the nineteenth century, underwent a spiritual resurrection that changed the course of his life. Having been arrested for belonging to a group judged treasonous by the czar, Dostoevsky was sentenced to death before a firing squad.

Czar Nicholas I carefully staged the execution scene, a grisly royal joke. Each conspirator was dressed in a white gown, bound, and led blindfolded to the public square, where a firing squad and a gawking crowd awaited them. Then at the last possible instant, a horseman galloped up with a message from the czar: The sentence of death would be mercifully commuted to hard labor.

Dostoevsky never recovered from the impact of his liberation. Now that he had escaped from death's iron grip, life became precious beyond measure. Believing that God had given him a second chance, he devoted himself to studying the New Testament and the lives of the saints. He emerged from prison with unshakable Christian convictions, and went on to write some of the most profound literature of his age. It is said that as long as the writings of Tolstoy and Dostoevsky exist in Russian literature, the witness of an incarnate God cannot be escaped.

Not all of us have stared death directly in the face, but we all live, nevertheless, with an underlying consciousness of its hovering presence. We hurry about, as if our haste would somehow postpone our mortal destiny. Our clocks and calendars monitor and mock us in our stride.

Behind the ordinary circumstances and comments of life exists the knowledge that our time is limited. Like a mother calling her children while they are at play, death will soon gather us from our sand piles to depart. Death is the final curtain, an imminent presence forcing us to assess the meaning and value of existence itself. Life is too short to be squandered.

The Bible uses the rather sobering metaphor of a mist in the air to describe life's brevity. "You are just a vapor that appears for a little while and then vanishes away" (James 4:14). Have you ever breathed on a cold windowpane and watched how quickly the fog on the pane evaporates into thin air? Such is the fleeting span of a person's lifetime.

All of life can be divided into two simple categories: the perishable and the imperishable. Christians are redeemed not by elements of the temporal realm like silver and gold but by the imperishable blood of Christ. God wants to turn our attention to what is lasting, what has permanent value because it is a reflection of His own nature.

Even within the earthly realm we prefer gold to tin, marble to wood. Almost every object has a certain worth based on the illusion of durability and permanence. In a much truer sense, God determines something's value by its eternal significance. We know from Scripture that God's Word, His Kingdom, and the souls of all people will remain after all the rest is a smoking heap of rubble. But is that all? What becomes of the everyday aspects of life, such as washing the car or typing your son's English theme? Are all these lost in a sea of temporal meaninglessness?

You are perhaps familiar with the common refrain, "Only one life, 'twill soon be past; Only what's done for Christ will last." The implications of this statement are that *everything* done for Christ will last. Whatever originates from the flesh is fleshly; but what originates from the Spirit is spiritual (John 3:6). In other words, not the activity itself but its *source* determines its eternal value.

If you are abiding in Christ, then you can lead a Bible study *and* overhaul a car with equal assurance that your actions are eternally significant—which is no mere academic point if you are struggling with the purpose and meaning of life. We need to remember that God will bring every act to judgment, both good and bad (Ecclesiastes 12:14). Everything you do will be weighed on the scales of eternity. To misconstrue this concept might produce the dichotomous notion that "secular" work cannot be made truly spiritual except at those points where you are sharing Christ or inviting a friend to church. You are then left with a fragmented, splintered existence in which only overtly spiritual activities have meaning.

God offers us a purpose-filled, integrated life. He is more than willing to help us discern what shape that life should take for each of us individually. He is the God who says, "I am the LORD your God, who teaches you to profit, who leads you in the way you should go" (Isaiah 48:17). As a result of such a sense of purpose in our lives, we should be able to say with confidence, "This is what I want to give myself to," or, "This is a waste of time."

Numbering our days

The Death of a Salesman by Arthur Miller portrays Willy Loman, a traveling salesman whose aim in life is to make it big, to have everybody like him, to see his sons follow in his steps. One by one, his dreams are all shattered. First he loses his job. And then he realizes, much to his dismay, that his sons mirror all his insecurities.

Willy finally commits suicide in despair. The play ends by his graveside with his son's revelation: "He had the wrong dreams. . . . He never knew who he was." Perhaps Willy never really stopped to define his dreams, to admit that what he was living for was unworthy of such uncommon effort. Futile dreams lead to bankrupt lives.

How do we avoid Willy's kind of desperation? How do we get off the never-ending treadmill—the monotonous grind of going to school in order to graduate and get a job so that we can get married and have children who will go to school to get a job . . . and on and on. We sometimes make the statement, "He spent his life" doing such and such. Indeed, life is spent, invested, exchanged for what we consider to be important. We all have a *life purpose,* even if that purpose is never articulated. Our reason for living might even be as mundane as playing golf. But whatever our purpose in life may be, it determines the way we spend our days. Thus, our daily activities usually reveal our life purpose.

If we would like to look back someday on a life well spent, then we must prayerfully consider what we should be doing right now. If you wanted to articulate and record your life purpose and related goals, how would you go about it? Here are a few suggestions.

The first step might be to think over the last few weeks or months or years, and then answer the question, "In view of how I have used that time, what am I really living for, what is my purpose in life?" If the answer to this question is difficult to discern, try asking a good friend or your spouse this question: "By the way I live my life in your presence, what do you think I am living for? What is really important to me?" Most people find this self-realization and feedback very revealing. One friend admitted, "When I forced myself to articulate my goals, I found that deep down my real purpose in life was to do better than my Dad. I wanted to prove myself, and the only way I knew how was to get a better car or job or house."

As you can see, this whole process is wasted effort unless you are thoroughly willing to be honest with yourself. It is said that the statement "God loves me and has a wonderful plan for my life" can easily degenerate into "God loves me and I sure hope He approves of my plan." The question is, What does God want from my life?

The next step, then, is to prayerfully formulate a life purpose that reflects biblical values. Your life purpose is a statement of what you intend to live for or invest your life in. It's the ideal you keep in your mind as the end result of all your action and effort, all the while acknowledging that it probably won't be totally accomplished in your lifetime. Ask yourself questions like these that get right to the heart of the matter: Could I still hold to this life purpose if I were to develop a debilitating illness? Does this purpose enable me to play out all of life's scenes with continuity and meaning? Does this life purpose have biblical authenticity?

If you were to state, "My life purpose is to know and obey God by applying His Word to my life," then you would have an ideal to aim toward all your life. It would be necessary to consider this broad purpose in every major area of responsibility in your life: your family, work, ministry, lifestyle, walk with God, relationship to the Body, and relationship to the unbelieving world.

You might want to force yourself to attach the simple word "by" to your statement of purpose. For instance, you might say, "I want to glorify God in my family *by* becoming a godly, sensitive husband and father." Or, "I want to glorify God by maintaining a lifestyle that strives toward simplicity and allows freedom for ministry to people."

How you define your life purpose can vary greatly, depending on your individual gifts and calling. A person who senses God leading him to take an aggressive leadership role in battling abortion and pornography should reflect that calling in his life purpose. If God has given you the gift of helps, you may want to define your lifestyle with extra flexibility, maintaining an "on-call" status with other people. Because we all grow in our understanding of our individual gifts and calling, we should try to refine and clarify our life purposes on a regular basis, perhaps yearly.

Defining life purposes can be a liberating release from entanglements that often pull us off course—that is, provided we know what course we are on. Paula and I have a penchant for old houses, the kind where you can smell gingerbread and cinnamon between the cracks in the oak. We would have bought one long ago, except that the necessary renovation process would detract from the simple, more available lifestyle spelled out in our life purposes. If, however, our gifts were to include hospitality and if we could envision such a time investment contributing toward the ministry

God has called us to, then we would welcome the thought of rejuvenating an old house. Defining life purposes helps us more quickly realize what does and doesn't "fit."

Going through this process has had a pronounced effect on my life, helping me clarify and provide the parameters for what God has called me to. It has helped answer this difficult question: Of all the things I *could* conceivably do, what *should* I do? What is the most strategic use of my time and effort? The act of writing and rewriting purposes and goals has a built-in accountability factor. I find myself going back to what I wrote and deciding that I must either erase it or begin to practice it. As one businessman said to me, "I stated and restated and clarified my purposes and goals until I was truly committed to them."

Off the paper and into your life

Once you have articulated your life purpose, the next step of establishing goals follows naturally. *Goals* are short-term, measurable objectives that reflect your larger life purposes. They enable you to reject the superfluous, and then to concentrate on the direction in which God is leading you. They make it possible for a life purpose to hop off the paper and into your life.

You can state a goal in terms of any time length that seems reasonable. It is especially helpful to differentiate between five-year and one-year goals, since there are some priorities you will not be able to address for at least a year.

Bringing a life purpose down to measurable

goals keeps you honest with yourself. I have a business student friend who once shared with me how he hoped to get a high-paying job in order to carry out the larger life purpose of giving generously to Christian causes. He then sheepishly admitted upon my prompting that he was not giving anything at the present time. He had never taken the second step of establishing short-term goals to reach this long-term life purpose. I shared with him the observation that those who give a little when they have a little are usually the same ones who give generously when their income increases.

We readily associate setting goals with many areas of life—losing weight, gaining new clients, increasing sales, learning a new skill. But isn't it a strange paradox how reticently we approach goal setting in a realm that seems far more spiritual, such as prayer and evangelism, as though these things "just happen" without any planning or forethought?

A friend once recounted how she started selling toys through home parties in order to provide additional income and meet nonChristians. "It was easy," she said, "to aim for a certain level of sales per month. But I found that unless I determined to have a woman over for coffee or lunch regularly, I never reached my goal of getting to know nonChristians and sharing the gospel with them." We cannot expect spiritual growth and fruitfulness to occur magically without consistent application of our motivational drive and the setting of goals.

A word of caution

Whenever the subject of setting goals and living by priorities is broached, something in us reacts. We form the caricature of a stopwatch inside our head that prompts us to interrupt the person we're talking to mid-sentence, causing us to say, "I'm sorry, but you'll have to tell me about your mother's death later. It doesn't fit into my schedule today."

But living with purpose does not eliminate spontaneity or the relaxation of lingering over a cup of coffee. A purposeful life is not lived at such a frenzied pitch that every hour is like a hamster's jaw that we cram full with as much as we can. Furthermore, living a purposeful life is not like writing a script God is somehow obligated to follow, as though my fine but fleshly efforts could guarantee the realized goal. God has His own ways of keeping us flexible and dependent on Him in our planning. After all, "The mind of man plans his way, but the LORD directs his steps" (Proverbs 16:9).

To live purposefully is to live as Jesus lived, with a clear sense of direction and calling. He extricated Himself from the clinging multitudes who would have gladly made Him a cult personality. Even His closest friends could not deter Him from His mission. He lived from the center outward. His eyes were riveted toward the Cross.

Or we might want to reflect on what Paul said of his own life: "I do not consider my life of any account as dear to myself, in order that I may finish my course, and the ministry which I received from the Lord Jesus, to testify solemnly of the gospel of the grace of God" (Acts 20:24). Paul knew what course he was on, and he was prepared to sacrifice toward that end.

In the idealistic dreams of our twenties, we have the illusion we can do and be anything if we just try hard enough. Few doors seem closed to us. But in this process of defining life purposes and short-term goals, we are closing the door on some options, even as we say yes to others. Medical students who purposefully choose to be family doctors in order to have more time and availability to people must be prepared to see their surgeon friends driving Mercedes. Mothers who invest quality time and effort in their children may lag behind in an outside career field. When we establish purposes and priorities before God, we must make difficult choices.

If someday we sit in the rocking chair of our old age and look back on life with regret, with a sense of having wandered aimlessly over a faceless terrain, it will be because we never stopped long enough to assess our direction or because we chose to give ourselves to empty dreams.

In our culture's preoccupation with *now* lies a denial of the past and a refusal to face the future. But God has designed us to live in the present with our eyes on both. He has saved us in the past and promises us a future too wonderful to comprehend. God can give meaning and direction to the present, but only as we determine to live with purpose—for Him.

8
Money: What's It Worth?

> He who has God and everything has no more than he who has God alone.
>
> *C. S. Lewis*

This generation, perhaps more than any other in this century, will be forced to wrestle with the value we attach to money—the "stuff of life." We are wedged between a dazzling array of consumer options and the sober knowledge of our spiritual responsibility to a lost and needy world. Is money something dangerous and dirty that inevitably corrupts, or is it really worth something in the Kingdom of God?

Before packing the last boxes for the moving van, Ted and Janet took one more look around their home. Janet's eyes surveyed the spacious kitchen with custom cabinets and pantry she had yet to fill. She fondly remembered the occasions when groups of twenty or more were easily fed in the large dining area. Ted admired again the cathedral ceiling and rich woodwork that made their family antiques look right at home. Without voicing the thought aloud, each of them wondered whether they could afford a house so well tailored to their needs and desires when they reached their next location.

It's not as if they hadn't weighed heavily the costs of moving. The prospects of a new job and new opportunities with people, however, overshadowed the discomfort and uncertainty of uprooting a family.

The first few weeks in their new location confirmed their fears. Housing prices were twenty percent higher. That blunt fact, along with higher interest rates, forced Ted and Janet to one conclusion: Either they would have to be content with a much smaller house or they would have to bring in additional income, an unacceptable alternative because of time demands.

They came to this realization reluctantly, as they envisioned furniture crowded into a smaller, tract home. Ted summed it up when he said, "We came here because we felt God would give us a spiritual ministry with people in this job and place. Now we have the chance to put to the test what we've always said: that our material position in life isn't all that important."

Sometimes we have the urge to just pick up and move to another culture where we'd be so thankful to have curtains that it wouldn't matter if they matched the bedspread; where we would be thrilled to have *any* sort of motorized transportation.

Consider St. Francis of Assisi, who, renouncing all earthly possessions, once walked naked down the street proclaiming his freedom from the tyranny of things. In some ways, voluntary poverty might appear to be the easiest step: no budgets, bank accounts, or credit cards to manage. Yet even this prospect offers no guarantees, no assurance of freedom from unrealistic expectations about possessions and money.

Money and the Kingdom needs

The temptation to accumulate can hardly be overstated. Karl Marx taught that in our world people exist because of what they have. Thus, if they have nothing, they do not exist. We see this materialist philosophy today reshaped and touted under a slightly more subtle suggestion: You are what you own. "The more you own, the more you are."[1] "How much is he worth?" we ask. In practically every culture, so the saying goes, "Money talks." In ours, it is the mother tongue.

We in the Christian community are not immune. William Murray, in his book *My Life Without God,* recounts what life was like as Madalyn Murray O'Hair's son. He recalls how his mother's tirade against God began in the Baltimore courts as she sought to have prayer removed from the local public school. Anticipating vehement opposition, Mrs. O'Hair and her family were amazed that no Christian group came forward to file a dissenting argument. Not long thereafter, she moved to have the tax exempt status lifted from Baltimore clergy. The Christian community rose up in arms. There are few injuries felt deeper than those dealt our pocketbooks.

But we should not be surprised. Money is not portrayed in the Bible as a neutral entity, a passive tool in our hands to be used for good or ill. Money is a rival god. You cannot serve both God and Mammon, we are told (Matthew 6:24). Having a seductive power all its own, money is capable of inspiring devotion, of giving us a false sense of security, freedom, and omnipotence. It takes on the very characteristics of deity, tempting us to solicit from inferior sources what God has always offered freely.[2]

Yet all is not lost. Money does have spiritual value. In certain ways, money can be invested toward eternal, lasting wealth. For there are many real physical needs that exist in the spiritual Kingdom of God. "Lay up for yourselves treasures in heaven, where neither moth nor rust destroys, and where thieves do not break in or steal" (Matthew 6:20). Rather than becoming a servant to money, we can *use* it redemptively for eternal investments in people, in furthering the Kingdom.

There is only one major problem. I can sit on a new sofa, but what of treasures in heaven, treasures the Bible does not even describe? Perhaps this is why Christ's familiar teaching about treasures, money, and anxiety also includes this succinct verse about spiritual sight: "If therefore your eye is clear, your whole body will be full of light" (Matthew 6:22). It takes spiritual vision to see the paradox: What looks permanent is actually passing away, but what is truly real we see only by faith. Yet if I lack that spiritual sight, why would I want to use money for anything other than my own temporal pleasures?

We must have eyes to see. The money we exchange for the pizza served to our neighbors builds relationships with *people*, opening a door for the gospel to come to them. Or consider the example of our friend John. He invested money in an airplane ticket to visit a friend who had strayed from God. He felt compelled to make this trip because long ago he and his friend had carved their names and a verse in a rock, commemorating their prayer that God would give them each a wife. Now, years later, his friend had left this very wife. John was hoping to exchange his time and money to retrieve his brother.

Every so often we need to be reminded what is really important. Stacy and I were once invited to a lovely English Tudor home for the rehearsal dinner of a wedding he was to perform. As soon as we drove up, I realized we were about to step inside a fashionable magazine cover. As we toured the home, I marveled at the perfect attention to detail, the sheer beauty of period antiques, brass, and baby's breath.

I happened to sit beside an old friend who filled me in on all that God had been doing in her life in recent years. She related how God had multiplied the feeble efforts of our joint Bible study venture among her friends. Some of the women from this Bible study had now led other friends to Christ.

Although I thoroughly enjoyed the remainder

of the evening inside someone else's elegant home, God used this conversation to rub off some of the luster. As I sat there overlooking the pool, I realized that here, in God's work in this woman and her friends, was real wealth. If it were a question of having to choose between spiritual wealth in people and material wealth in things, then the choice, seen from the right perspective, was fairly simple.

Money and the Kingdom within

So money can be a medium of exchange or a means of investing in matters of lasting, eternal value. When we place money in an offering plate or write a check to a missionary board or take a nonChristian neighbor's children to the zoo, do we see all that is really taking place? God uses the act of giving, of exchanging money, for eternal things—to further His Kingdom not only in the world but in *us* as well.

Jeremiah described Israel at the nadir of its culture in this way: "From the least even to the greatest every one is greedy for gain" (Jeremiah 8:10). In the New Testament, the spiritual leader was to be free from the love of money, not attracted by "sordid gain" (1 Peter 5:2). Everywhere you turn in Scripture, making money unjustly and hoarding it are condemned.

God established giving, at least in part, as a drain plug for man's greed. We give, not because God needs the gift but because we need to give. Jesus allowed the women who accompanied Him and His disciples to contribute financially to their ministry, which is not surprising until you stop to think of how He fed the five thousand. Obviously, Christ could easily have "paid" His own way!

Financial sacrifice in the Old Testament was set in the context of spiritual feast days, as part of the joy of being called out of the world as God's people. Jews under the law were instructed to tithe ten percent of their income to the Levites, ten percent for a sacred feast day, and another ten percent every third year for those who were fatherless, strangers, or widows. The Old Testament standard for giving was not the ten percent normally associated with tithing but an average of twenty-two percent a year.

The New Testament indicates that giving under grace is to be generous, proportionate to one's income, and individually determined before God. Giving is both an act of submitting to His ownership and a declaration of our freedom from servitude to a false god. Thereby God meets our deepest needs, which are not food and clothes but freedom and hope. The first step toward that freedom is the releasing, the unclinching of the hand that holds our wealth.

"As a young Christian, I was so tight I squeaked," one Christian shared. "But as I grew spiritually, I came to realize that God had given me the spiritual gift of giving. I love to give now. But the first step in that direction was believing that God had given me my abilities and opportunities to be used for Him. The next step was being released from debilitating worry and anxiety about money. The fear of not having enough money made the act of giving a painful ordeal rather than spiritual liberation."

God wants your heart. But the heart can go in different directions. A person's deepest affections and attachments indicate the path to his greatest treasure. What you do with your wealth is not only a mirror of the heart within but can also be a means of centering the heart on God. Hoarding or withholding wealth causes a corrosion of values, the diminishing of relationships, a shriveling of the soul.

A successful businessman explained to us how God has led him to place a ceiling on his income, thereby circumventing any tendency to grasp and accumulate. From all income over the fixed amount he has set to meet his family's needs, he gives an increasing percentage to whatever outside need God presents. "The exciting part," he said, "is seeing God match the amount with the need, time after time."

What we do with our wealth is not the only spiritual concern, however. As Francis Schaeffer wrote only a few months before he died, "When Christians get to heaven and they speak of how much they gave to missions, to build schools, and so on, [I think] the Lord is going to tell them it would have been better if they had had less money to give and had made their money with justice."[3] No amount of money given to Christian causes can cleanse the corruption from money made at other people's expense, of wealth accumulated by sacrificing the well-being of family, fellow workers, or one's own health.

Corrie Ten Boom tells this story about her watchmaker father, Casper. The Ten Boom family once prayed that God would send someone that very day to purchase a watch that would pay their bills due at the bank. In walked a customer with a roll of cash and the need of a good quality watch. Just as the man purchased an expensive watch, he began to complain about a Christian watchmaker friend of Casper's from whom he felt he had received poor service.

Casper asked if he could see this watch that was not running properly. It needed only a minor repair, which Casper made, assuring the customer that the other watchmaker had sold him a good watch and could be trusted. The amazed gentleman returned the new watch he had just bought and Casper returned his money.

"Papa, why did you do that? Aren't you worried about the bills you have due?" Corrie asked him impatiently as soon as the man had gone.

"There is blessed and unblessed money," her father replied. God would not be glorified in the ruined reputation of another Christian. He would not contribute to that. A few days later, another man came to their shop and bought the most expensive watch made at the time, enabling them to pay their bills and to send Corrie for two years watchmaking training in Switzerland.

Perhaps the greatest safeguard in managing money and controlling greed is what few of us have: a friend or spiritual mentor who will hold us accountable and give us trustworthy advice. It is said that personal finances, like sex in earlier generations, is the new forbidden subject of discussion. The attitude that "what I do with my money is my private business" prevails. What each of us needs, though, is someone who can help us discern at critical junctures, "Is this new opportunity a temptation to avoid or a blessing from the Lord?"

The cornerstone of contentment

"There are two ways to get enough," G. K. Chesterton once said. "One is to continue to accumulate more and more and the other is to desire less." Giving is like an inverted savings program: We find as we participate in giving that God shrinks our mercenary desires. Giving tames our lusts.

"Godliness with contentment is great gain" (1 Timothy 6:6, NIV). It is the freedom to concentrate on more important things, the ability to say, "This is enough. I don't need one more winter sweater, one more kitchen gadget, or fifty more feet of lawn to mow."

The appropriate banner to hang outside the average after-Christmas sale might be the verse, "For all these things the Gentiles *eagerly* seek" (Matthew 6:32, italics added). With faces drawn and purses clutched tightly, shoppers barge and elbow their way through the crowds.

Yet God promises to meet our needs. One of our greatest needs is to be freed from that frantic I've-got-to-get-this-now feeling. Over the years, I've learned as a keen homemaker-consumer to take an inside barometer reading of "shopping anxiety." Invariably I make poor judgments in that pressurized state, so if I just relax, the Lord brings my way what I truly need.

A friend who is a real-estate developer in the Southwest invests a great deal of time helping Christians with the stewardship of their finances. "People should always live at a lower standard of living," he says, "than what they can actually afford. This enables them to give and save. It also insures a good testimony before unbelievers and other Christians." He likes to quote Aristotle's statement, "It is good for a man's soul to know what he can do without."

This friend encourages Christians to consider this question about lifestyle witness in their purchases, especially the major ones like houses and cars: "What impact will this purchase have on the Great Commission and on my part in that commission?" He uses the example of a surgeon friend who struggled with which house he should buy. He knew that he could afford a very large, expensive home, but he eventually decided on a more moderate choice so that he would not limit his ability to help other men spiritually. He did not want to present them with a well-to-do model they might always strive to copy.

All of us need to see concrete ways in which God supplies our needs. Stacy once taught a class of deeply committed laymen and their wives. His subject was "Claiming God's Promises." About midway through the session, he had us list specific Bible promises we could claim. Everyone in the class could readily share appropriate verses about assurance of salvation and forgiveness of sin. They were certain of eternal life. When it came to promises for God's guidance, there was again no lack of ready references.

Then he came to the area that both of us thought would be the easiest: God's promises to provide for His children. But there were long, awkward pauses. Finally, Stacy broke the silence, mentioning the promise in Philippians 4:19: "My God shall supply all your needs according to His riches in glory in Christ Jesus." After a few more minutes of waiting, I threw one out to punctuate the nervous silence. Then Stacy waited again, and stated another verse. Finally, when it almost seemed that he and I were the only ones who had been forced to claim God's promises to provide, Stacy moved on to another topic.

"Living by faith" is not a phrase reserved for pastors and missionaries. We need to be able to tell our children, "We prayed that God would lead us to the right house [or the right car, or the right tutoring program], and this is the one He provided." We fall too easily into the habit of seeing something we think we need, and then instantly writing out a check for it—without prayer, without planning, without giving God the chance to direct us.

I find myself often returning, in my personal life, to God's message to rich people, a category that applies to most of us in the Western world. We who have more than we really need are called to fix our hope on Him, not on what we own. The Lord wants us to be generous and ready to share, "storing up . . . the treasure of a good foundation for the future, [taking hold] of that which is life indeed" (1 Timothy 6:19). God appeals to us with the prospect of exchanging the materialistic illusion of wealth for a solid foundation of Life.

Christ came to give us *eternal* life, of which there is inherently none in money and material things. I take comfort in the fact that even if we could afford a new mini-van instead of a used station wagon, next week something else would try to seduce us with an empty promise to satisfy that seemingly inconsolable longing within.

Only God's eternal presence can effectively fill the void. All other attempts satisfy only for a moment. As C. S. Lewis said, "Our Father refreshes us on the journey with some pleasant inns, but will not encourage us to mistake them for home."[4]

Notes

1. Indirectly quoted by Tom Sine, *The Mustard Seed Conspiracy* (Waco: Word, 1981), page 31. He footnotes William Irwin Thompson, *Darkness and Scattered Light* (Garden City, N. Y.: Doubleday & Co., Anchor Press, 1978), page 67.
2. See *Money, Sex & Power* by Richard Foster (San Francisco: Harper & Row, 1985), pages 25-35, and *Money and Power* by Jacques Ellul (Downers Grove: Inter-Varsity Press, 1984) for a more thorough discussion.
3. Francis Schaeffer, *The Great Evangelical Disaster* (Westchester: Crossway Books, 1984), page 116.
4. C. S. Lewis, *The Problem of Pain,* page 115.

9
A Matter of Perspective

Let temporal things serve your use, but the eternal be the object of your desire.

Thomas à Kempis

A person who is under an illusion actually thinks he is being realistic. He doesn't recognize that he has a false picture of reality. What kind of perspective on life creates the illusion that the material universe is all there is? Why do so many people limit their lives in a pursuit of material reality without giving a serious thought to spiritual reality? Esau was under this kind of illusion.

Esau was a man with many built-in advantages. He enjoyed all the privileges of being Isaac's eldest son. His life had been consecrated to God from birth. As the firstborn, he could look forward to special spiritual position someday within his family and culture. He knew that God had sworn to bless all the nations of the earth through his grandfather Abraham's seed. From Esau's perspective, he was the legitimate heir of those promises.

Esau was known as "a man of the field," a hairy outdoorsman who loved the exhilaration of the hunt and its reward, the savory taste of game. But the fact was that he loved both too much.

One day Esau came in from his hunting, famished from his exploits. Jacob, his brother, noticed Esau's hunger and seized the opportunity. He proposed a simple trade: Esau's birthright in exchange for his lentil stew. Esau agreed. What good was a birthright, he reasoned, if he were dead from hunger? (Genesis 25:27-34).

If this sketch were performed as a play, at this point we would hear a gasp from the audience. No, Esau. Surely you would not let go of your birthright for a bowl of stew. The audience would wait for Esau to retract his request, to come to his senses. But Esau's blunder was no slip of the tongue in a moment of extremity. It was the result of a lifetime of feeding his appetite, of profaning the holy.

Esau was a typical materialist. He willingly exchanged the spiritual for the sensual, the eternal for the temporal, what he could not see for what he could. He thus profaned and discarded his birthright.

When Jacob eventually cheated him out of his father's blessing as well, Esau showed some evidence of remorse. We can feel his anguish when he cries out "with an exceedingly great and bitter cry . . . 'Bless me, even me also, O my Father!'"

(Genesis 27:34). But it was too late; he had already made his choice.

Esau would have felt right at home in the twentieth century. Ours is a materialistic world, not just in our drive to accumulate but in a much deeper sense: in our inability to perceive what is real and valuable. Modern man is like Orual in C. S. Lewis's book *Till We Have Faces*. Orual asks her tutor, "You don't think, not possibly—not a mere hundredth chance—there might be things that are real though we can't see them?"[1]

All that is human in man desperately longs to believe that there is. He reaches for some transcendent truth, for something "out there" that will save him from the endless silence of the grave into which all life's noble and mundane deeds tumble. For deep down, he knows that if it all comes to nothing, his existence itself is "an exquisite cheat."[2]

Without that outside reference point, man has no dependably solid base on which to build a life of meaning. His choice, as Camus insisted, is either suicide or the courageous effort to "authenticate" his existence, to live as though there were meaning and purpose to life while knowing full well there is none.

Such is the inherent despair of the person who believes that this world is all there is. He can see the form but not the substance, the event without the meaning. People become statistics, families turn out to be just mix-and-match clusters of people under one roof, and sex assumes the casual, ephemeral air of an afternoon's romp in the park. In what distant, archaic land do values such as honesty, courtesy, and fidelity dwell?

As Christians, we breathe a sigh of relief to be free of such despair and folly. This world, we insist, is not all there is. It both cloaks and reveals something about the eternal realm. In the very act of coming to Christ, we are acknowledging the supernatural, the transcendent, the eternal Reference Point. We place our faith in Someone we have never met, and accept His payment for the unseen, fallen nature harbored deep within. We have been cleansed from sins we could never measure and initiated into a Kingdom not yet fully revealed.

Unfortunately, many of us suffer from a serious inconsistency between theory and practice. Although we believe deeply in the unseen spiritual world, we nonetheless build our lives upon the same materialistic principles held by any modern unbeliever. In his book *True Spirituality,* Francis Schaeffer spoke of two men sitting back-to-back in separate chairs. One (the non-Christian) sees only the natural part of the universe, and the other (the Christian) faces the total reality of not only the supernatural, unseen world but also the natural, visible one. Each defines and lives out truth against the kind of background he sees.[3]

Unfortunately, Christians often end up living, in practical terms, in the position of the materialist (Schaeffer called this the "chair of unfaith"). Even though we sing "I Need Thee Every Hour" on Sunday morning, we make decisions, fashion ambitions, and define the parameters of daily, hourly life as though the eternal and the supernatural did not even exist.

When this kind of compromise takes place, our lives no longer exude the pleasant aroma or demonstrate the effective power of the risen Christ, no matter how flawless our theology may seem to be. The ceiling is too low; there is no room for God to intervene. Our mind-set is often much like that of Christ's disciples, who, when confronted with the problem of feeding five thousand hungry people, concluded immediately that they must be sent to the nearest restaurant. Without the spiritual resources that come from a life fully lived for Christ, we are just playing at the Christian life. The real battle is not against flesh and blood but against spiritual forces. That's why we must wage our warfare in the unseen, eternal realm of prayer closets, claimed promises, and perseverance.

If we as Christians are caught in the prevailing quagmire where reality is defined by our five senses, we will not be inclined to give our lives to the eternal. If we build our lives on a materialistic base, then when we find ourselves in some gray, antiseptic hospital room face-to-face with death, we will stumble across that mortal chasm only slightly better prepared than the nonChristian in the next bed.

Deception and its remedy

How does our vision become so clouded? Why is it that we believe the eternal, transcendent realm exists, and yet we live as though it does not? At least part of the answer can be found in the Old Testament god-makers, who insisted that reality must have shape and substance. When we read Isaiah's and Jeremiah's descriptions of those "who fashion graven images," our minds conjure up a primitive barbarian, knife-in-hand, carving a cypress tree into a figure before which he will prostrate himself in worship. We feel little in common with such a superstitious barbarian.

Yet the gods of modern men are only slightly less blatant. Instead of carved images in the shape of calves, we fashion images of ourselves. Instead of depending on the power behind a statue of molten gold, we depend on the power behind our wealth to deliver us. We put our hope in position and achievement to give us security and worth. Modern men may not slaughter animals or lay flowers before a statue, but we just as readily sacrifice family life, depth with God, and relationships with struggling unbelievers before the god of getting ahead. When we begin to make such sacrifices, our faith becomes bound up in this world. What is real and valuable to us is what we can see and experience now.

In the examples of both the primitive and the modern god-worshipers, there is a substitution of means for ends. The tree is useful as fuel for warmth or as a reminder of the One who made it. My wealth is a gift from a gracious God, a means of advancing His Kingdom. But to look to either for deliverance, as a manifestation of transcendent reality, is idolatry in the classic sense. As Augustine said, "Idolatry is worshiping anything that ought to be used, or using anything that is meant to be worshiped."

God could describe us with the same words He used to describe those of Jeremiah's day: "My people have committed two evils: They have forsaken Me, the fountain of living waters, to hew for themselves cisterns, broken cisterns, that can hold no water" (Jeremiah 2:13).

What an empty, desolate picture the Old Testament prophets paint of the person who looks to anything or anyone other than the living God for spiritual help. Such a person "feeds on ashes," Isaiah says. "A deceived heart has turned him aside. And he cannot deliver himself, nor say, 'Is there not a lie in my right hand?'" (Isaiah 44:20).

Such deception erodes our ability to perceive the lies we live with—lies that persuade us that wealth, status, stylish clothes, or some other standard of success in the material world can bring us the security and meaning we long for. The Lord says through Isaiah, "I have formed you, you are My servant. . . . I have wiped out your transgressions. . . . Return to Me, for I have redeemed you" (Isaiah 44:21-22).

How shall we return, and when we find our way Home, how will we remain? The Bible is a map for pilgrims trying to make their way through a barren land. Every time we open its pages we're reminded of the eternal realm, of the supernatural dimension hidden and revealed in the natural world.

Have you ever observed the process of a child learning to read? There are some children who suddenly come to their parents and read words and complete sentences as if they were born with a book in their hands. Most children, however, after the very same exposure to words and letters, still need someone to point out, "This is a *c* and this is an *a* and this is a *t*, and when we put these letters together and say their sounds, we read the word *cat*."

Likewise, in spiritual matters, most of us are slow learners. The Holy Spirit is our Teacher. As we read the Word, our Teacher points out what is real and what is worth giving our lives to. He opens our eyes. As a wise man once said, "When I saw, I reflected upon it; I looked, and received instruction" (Proverbs 24:32). We not only need to *see*; we need to *see through*.

Scripture directs us to the transcendent, describing the events of the unseen world that correlate with those of the visible one. Like a news commentator speaking for the sake of those who weren't there, the Bible tells us of Christ entering heaven, the greater tabernacle, to appear in God's presence on our behalf. We see in its pages angels who influence the affairs of nations, a cloud of witnesses observing our pilgrimage toward a Kingdom that cannot be shaken.

Assessing proper value

It is a mark of maturity to be able to see the transcendent. Somewhere between a child's seventh and eighth years, he develops the ability to move from the tangible to the abstract, from the story to the underlying principle. Sin is no longer just some dark blob inside, symbolized by black construction paper. It is the evil that separates me from God, causing me to walk in darkness.

Unless I would forever remain a child in the spiritual realm, I must allow Scripture to tutor me into the maturity of recognizing what is real, lasting, and eternally valuable.

Not always, but quite often, what is significant in God's eyes is something small, long-range, or even hidden. In a world where bigger is usually better, Christ injects His parables of the mustard seed, yeast, and salt—all common items whose influence is disproportionately greater than their size. Only those with a biblically-altered perspective of reality can detect what is spiritually valuable. Only people whose eyes have been trained can truly see.

The ideology perpetuated in the Soviet materialistic society, as Solzhenitsyn said, is invariably this: "The result is what counts."[4] No matter if you sacrifice a way of life, the integrity of the family, the spiritual health of the people—only the result counts. The state is quite willing to sacrifice intangible values because all that matters is quantitative, measurable results.

In Western culture, we add one more criterion: The results should be large enough to make us feel successful. Even spiritual ministries are often evaluated by the budget size, and whether the buildings are large and filled on Sunday.

But a ministry is not a business venture, nor is Christianity a statistically favorable religion. Of the four soils Jesus mentioned, only one bears prolific fruit. Christ healed ten lepers, but only one returned to thank Him. Nine others walked off the scene without so much as a backwards glance. Yet Jesus was undeterred. Had He determined the success of His earthly ministry by the number of people who enthusiastically embraced His teaching, He would have returned rather quickly to the carpenter's shop.

Statistics, quantity, and size are concepts that fit well into the world of ledger sheets and marketing strategies. They fare poorly, however, in the realm of people with eternal souls, a realm where the Shepherd would leave the ninety-nine to seek out the one who was lost. People cannot be hustled into the Kingdom of God. This is one reason, as Paul reminds us, that God rewards the laborers in His vineyard: not on the basis of visible results but according to their effort and toil. For it is *God* who brings the truly meaningful results (1 Corinthians 3:7-8).

Some of us who came to Christ in the 1960s thought we would change the whole world in our generation. We had visions of great throngs of people, cup in hand, waiting patiently for us to dispense the Water of Life. The world has long since slid into an abysmal state. We have personally lowered our expectations to helping a moderate number of individuals over the course of a lifetime. But the real question, the one that rescues us from disillusionment and feelings of failure, is this: Is that really a lowering? Is it a small and insignificant vision unworthy of real sacrifice? Not when we consider the One who reached a world with a handful of men, who constantly multiplies His own life in people, whether or not we happen to be around to tabulate the "results."

Looking at what cannot be seen

The writer of Hebrews speaks of Abel, Enoch, Noah, and Abraham as people who lived as virtual strangers on the earth because they saw, far off in the distance, God's promises and His overall plan (Hebrews 11:4-16). Living by faith requires a willingness to live obediently, believing God for the positive outcome. As Paul said, "If we hope for what we do not see, with perseverance we wait eagerly for it" (Romans 8:25).

The most significant things in life take place not in hours and days but over months and years. Parenting is a prime example, for children have always made poor hothouse plants. A well-nurtured relationship with just one child requires hours, even years, of flying kites, making play dough, and talking through problems—and years with hugs of appreciation few and far between.

Likewise, God does not fashion us into spiritual giants overnight. The spiritually mature person has been trained to discern good and evil through years of a steady diet and *practice* of the Word (Hebrews 5:14). We cannot come to Scripture expecting to plot our spiritual progress daily on a graph. There are many days when what we receive is more like a time-released capsule than a startling new revelation. God teaches us "line on line, line on line, a little here, a little there" (Isaiah 28:10). In creating a mature oak of righteousness, He is prepared to invest time and patience.

The ability to see long-range brings constancy in the face of discouragement. William Wilberforce received word that the British Parliament had abolished slavery as he lay on his deathbed, exhausted from fifty years struggling against that very evil. Cotton Mather prayed several hours every day for revival in the American colonies. The Great Awakening began the year he died. What might have happened, what might not have happened, without the perseverance of these men who believed God for the future?

God seems to do His greatest work quietly, off in a corner, veiled from human view. Samuel was sent to anoint one of Jesse's sons as king of Israel. David, the most unlikely of candidates for that position, was off tending sheep. But he was the one God had chosen. When God sent His own Son, He tucked Him away in a hillside manger in Bethlehem.

When God makes His home in our hearts, He begins to sweep out the dusty corners, to open the windows for fresh air, to reconstruct the rafters. Our character is constantly under reconstruction, a process that is sometimes very painful. Our church attendance is laudable and our efforts in evangelism are commendable, but God searches the inner, hidden recesses of the heart. Are we allowing Him to uproot and rebuild? Or are we chafing against the divine obstacles in our path, like an unbroken horse straining to be free of bit and bridle? How fares the interior weather of our souls?

Agents of change come in many forms and

ways, but as most married couples would attest, one very common shape is that of a husband or wife. Who has not had moments of wondering how two such vastly different people ever wound up together under the same roof? It would perhaps be easier, but unspeakably boring, to be married to a person who was your own reflection. But marriage brings a necessary internal revolution in the palace of the ego, the place where our character is formed.

> To open my heart to another person is to invite him into my own throne room to sit down on my very own throne, on the seat normally warmed by no one but myself. And to do that is to have the throne, the seat of the ego, rocked right off its foundations.[5]

By this and many other such means does God conform us to His image, giving us His true riches, the fruit of the Spirit: love, joy, kindness, patience, peace, goodness, and faithfulness. Every obedience to His prompting is, as C. S. Lewis said, "the capture of a strategic point from which, a few months later, you may be able to go on to victories you never dreamed of. An apparently trivial indulgence in lust or anger today is the loss of a ridge or railway line or bridgehead from which the enemy may launch an attack otherwise impossible."[6] Our character is the sum total of our responses to God's hidden, inner workings in our hearts.

People whose eyes can see beyond the tangible and the immediate can appreciate the spiritual value of what is small, long-range, or hidden. Esau, who could not see beyond what was right in front of him, was an immoral and godless man (Hebrews 12:16). He exchanged his birthright, his spiritual heritage, for a bowl of lentils.

But what of us? What is our birthright as Christians? God said to Abraham, "I will surely bless you, and I will surely multiply you." To the heirs of these promises God desires even more to show that His purposes of blessing and multiplication remain the same (Hebrews 6:14-17).

We are the heirs of those promises. God has promised us the pleasure of His company in a way Esau could never have known. The Lord has assured us of rich spiritual fruitfulness. Perhaps the greatest danger facing us is that we would cling to what is worthless while the eternal prize slips right through our fingers.

Notes

1. C. S. Lewis, *Till We Have Faces* (New York: Harcourt, Brace, Jovanovich, 1957), page 141.
2. Thomas Howard and J. I. Packer, *Christianity: The True Humanism* (Waco: Word, 1985), pages 45-48.
3. *True Spirituality* by Francis Schaeffer offers a more thorough discussion, (Wheaton: Tyndale House, 1971), pages 60-70.
4. Aleksandr Solzhenitsyn, *The Gulag Archipelago, II*, page 609.
5. Mike Mason, *The Mystery of Marriage* (Portland: Multnomah, 1985), page 37.
6. C. S. Lewis, *Mere Christianity*, page 117.

10
A Family Heritage

What a parent says to his children is not heard by the world, but it will be heard by posterity.

Jean Paul Eixhter

In mid-March, 1944, German soldiers entered a house in Holland and arrested Casper Ten Boom, four of his children, and one of his grandchildren. They were arrested for hiding and protecting Jewish people from the Nazis' efforts to kill them. Four of those arrested in the Ten Boom house died in prison. One, his daughter Corrie, went on to tell the world of God's grace even within Hitler's wretched concentration camps.

Yet Corrie's story, so well told in her book *The Hiding Place,* actually begins at least two generations before with her grandfather, Willem Ten Boom. Willem was a deeply committed layman, an elder in the Dutch Reformed Church. His thinking was greatly influenced by a close friend who was a converted Jewish lawyer. Together they started the Society for Israel, which met regularly to pray for Israel and the protection of the Jewish people.

Willem's son Casper grew up well-versed in God's promise to Abraham: "I will bless those who bless you" (Genesis 12:3). Casper was spoon-fed a love for the Jews from the time of his youngest years.

Casper's only son, also named Willem, developed such a love for the Jewish culture and people that during his teenage years he paid a Jewish boy to teach him the Hebrew language. As a young minister, he became absorbed in the question of anti-Semitism. His sermons and writings were a prophetic call on the Church's responsibility to the Jews. Willem foresaw and decried the first stirrings of anti-Semitism years before the full gust of hatred could be felt.

A hundred years after the elder Willem Ten Boom first opened his home for prayer for Israel, soldiers arrested six of his descendants in the same house where those prayer meetings began. Over a period of many years, God was giving a vision and a mission to the Ten Boom family as a spiritual heritage to pass on. As the psalmist says, "The lovingkindness of the LORD is from everlasting to everlasting on those who fear Him, *and His righteousness to children's children*" (Psalm 103:17-18, italics added).

Could it be that God desires to reach far into succeeding generations through your family? Through ours? We see God's intentions clearly in

Malachi in a passage on marriage: "Has not the LORD made them one? In flesh and spirit they are his. And why one? *Because he was seeking godly offspring"* (Malachi 2:15, NIV, italics added). (It is just this prospect of a godly seed that Satan seeks to thwart in the lives of single Christians. His intense attacks are designed to lead them into relationships with unbelievers or with half-hearted Christians.)

Every Christian family has the potential for an eternal impact in countless lives. Are we living and acting now in a way that will influence our children and our children's children for Christ? Will they be able to have an impact on those around them? Can we visualize the future possibilities that can be realized through a family spiritual heritage?

Such a thought is not only encouraging but also convicting. For our children might not only display a heart for missions or a hunger for the Scriptures but also our ill-bred temper or lack of discipline. This negative prospect has prompted us to pray that the Lord would apply His promise in Isaiah to our children:

> "'I will pour out My Spirit on your offspring,
> And My blessing on your descendants. . . .'
> This one will say, 'I am the LORD'S';
> And that one will call on the name of Jacob;
> And another will write on his hand,
>   'Belonging to the LORD,'
> And will name Israel's name with honor."
>
> (Isaiah 44:3-5)

Our obedience or disobedience to this commission from God can have profound repercussions on those who follow us. God told Isaac, "I will multiply your descendants . . . *because Abraham obeyed Me and kept My charge* . . ." (Genesis 26:4-5, italics added). Yet Solomon sowed the seeds of his own son's downfall because he ignored God's instruction by marrying foreign wives who worshiped idols. Those wives turned not only Solomon's heart but also the hearts of his children away from the Lord.

It is interesting to read the biographies of Christians whose family trees are filled with the heritage of committed believers. James Dobson tells of his great-grandfather, George McCluskey, who invested the hour from eleven to twelve o'clock each morning in intercessory prayer for his family. He asked God to bless not only his children but also the generations yet to be born. Dobson then describes the fascinating way God answered that prayer in the lives of McCluskey's children and grandchildren: "There have been times as I have sat on the platform of a large church, waiting to speak, that I have felt the presence of the old man. . . . It staggers the mind to realize that the prayer of this one man, spoken more than fifty years ago, reach across four generations of time and influence developments in my life today."[1]

Henrietta Mears was another believer who influenced a generation of Christian leaders through her teaching ministry at Hollywood Presbyterian Church. Billy Graham admitted that no woman other than his wife or mother has had more influence on him than Miss Mears. Yet many of her personal and spiritual traits were those of her grandparents, the heritage of a rich spiritual background.

Unfortunately, not every story ends so well. As many Christian parents can attest, some children grow up to reject the faith of their fathers. Both Karl Marx and Sigmund Freud grew up in devoutly Christian homes. Yet both left the world an intellectual legacy that has greatly contributed to the erosion of our society's moral and spiritual values. As adults, both seemed determined to mount a direct attack on religious faith, Marx concluding that religion was merely the "opiate of the masses," and Freud calling it the "universal, obsessional neurosis." Both died bitter, disillusioned men, bereft of any faith, still harboring unhealed conflicts with their fathers.

The literary giant Ernest Hemingway was born and reared in one of Chicago's leading evangelical families. However, as his writing career flourished, his personal life lay in shambles. Married four times, he trotted the globe as a animal-killing, bullfighting tough boy—a manic-depressive who ended his life with a shotgun blast. Hemingway was the tragedy of Christian parents he felt he could never please, whose religious convictions he could not embrace, although, as his writings demonstrate, he could also never quite escape.

We must remind ourselves of sobering examples like these, lest we forget that although God's intention is surely generations of people who will speak His name with honor, yet the opposite also looms as a viable possibility. James Dobson's father once wrote him this exhortation: "I have observed that the greatest delusion is to suppose that our children will be devout Christians simply because their parents have been, or that any of them will enter into the Christian faith in any other way than through their parents' deep travail of prayer and faith."[2] We cannot assume that our children will instinctively inherit a deep faith just as automatically as they acquire our surname.

Fostering faith and biblical values

Every generation faces the challenge to pass on a biblical faith to the following generation, just as one relay runner hands the baton to the next. After God's people had crossed into the Promised Land, Joshua erected twelve stones from the Jordan River as a visual object lesson for the next generation to remind them of all God had done. Joshua said to the people of Israel, "When your children ask their fathers in time to come, saying, 'What are these stones?' then you shall inform your children, saying, 'Israel crossed this Jordan on dry ground' . . . that all the peoples of the earth may know that the hand of the LORD is mighty . . ." (Joshua 4:21-24). Each of us needs tangible, thought-through means of imparting to our children what God has done not only in our lives but in the history of God's people as well.

This is why we tell Bible stories to our children, giving them snapshots of people whose lives reveal God's faithfulness. Each story is the stone of a memory with which to build confidence in God's character. Through this process we can teach our children that just as God helped a young boy slay a giant with a slingshot, He can help them as well.

Joshua's memorial stones set a precedent for us that should stimulate creative thinking. One couple we know keeps a scrapbook for each child, to be given to the child on his thirteenth birthday. Inside is the record of significant family and personal events, as well as answers to corporate prayer. As each child then enters his teen years, he has a clear reminder of the Christian heritage of his family.

In the life of every child and teenager, moments of special receptivity arise. If we are attentive, we can capture those moments and tailor the Truth to his individual needs. He may know the story of Daniel in the lion's den by heart, but in his own personal times of testing he probably needs someone to help him make the correlation, to remind him that God delivers.

Yet Christian teaching, for all its worth, is only half the story. Our real values, the way we *live*, must be congruent with the Christian message we espouse. Inevitably, our "informal curriculum," what we teach by our behavior, speaks louder than our "formal curriculum," the message we articulate. For instance, if we quietly and inconspicuously circumvent the law, our children conclude that "secret sins" are permissible. If every trial and difficulty is cause for frustration and despair, then obviously difficulties are to be avoided at all costs.

What we really believe to be important in life will come through to our children. As in a magazine advertisement, the subliminal message behind our words and actions is inescapable. Christian counselor Lawrence Crabb makes this very point:

> Make no mistake. Children will in some form reproduce our efforts to find significance and security. If we really believe that money and achievement bring significance or that compliments and attractive clothing bring security, we can prate all we want about the joys of knowing Jesus. Our kids will learn to depend on what we really are depending on for our satisfaction in life. No amount of teaching, family devotions, or trips to church will effectively counter the message we convey with our lives.[3]

In most cultures, a certain form of outward talent and beauty are highly prized. But God values inner beauty, Christ-like character. A friend with an unusually lovely daughter explained the inward cringe he feels when people say to him within her hearing, "What a beautiful daughter you have." He has learned that he must be quick to add, "But you know what we really appreciate about her is her *inner* beauty, her attitude and outlook on life." He knows the importance of helping her place a higher value on something of lasting, eternal worth rather than emphasizing the fleeting advantage of physical beauty.

Raising children for God is a challenge in an affluent culture. A rather wealthy friend described an incident in his family that illustrates his effort to communicate biblical values on money to his children. His oldest son once came to him for the money for some designer jeans twice the price of regular, good quality ones. He gently turned down his son's request. "But, Dad," his son replied, "we can afford it. Why not?"

His father went on to explain to him that what you can afford is not the only criterion for the purchases you make. Yes, he could afford to buy the jeans—even the store they came from, and perhaps the shopping center where the store was located. "But I want you to understand, Son," he said, "that in this family, we operate on the basis of being conservative with ourselves, and responsible but generous with others. You can buy jeans that will wear just as well without the label."

Our children are deeply affected by our attitudes toward other people. Family counselor and speaker J. Allan Petersen once remarked that he attributed the strong social consciousness of his boys, their concern for others' needs, to his wife's gift of hospitality. "We've had hundreds of people in and through our home. My wife used to have luncheons: one week for all the divorced women she knew, the next for all the widows. Our kids have grown up on that." Henrietta Mears credited her heart for people to her wealthy parents' habit of inviting not just relatives but also lonely, needy people to share their table and home.

We read in the Old Testament that God responded to His people's faithfulness to His values and precepts with His blessing on their descendants. Isaiah states of those who "love justice" and "hate robbery in the burnt offering" as the Lord does that "their offspring will be known among the nations. . . . All who see them will recognize them because they are the offspring whom the LORD has blessed" (Isaiah 61:8-9). David says of the righteous man, "All day long he is gracious and lends; *and his descendants are a blessing*" (Psalm 37:26, italics added).

A ministering family

As we recoil from a decadent culture that has rejected Christian faith and principles, the temptation is to draw our children tightly about us. Our fear of losing them can make us turn inward in self-protection at the very point where God would have us set our light on a hill.

We sometimes get so caught up in the privilege and optimism of being part of a Christian family that we lose sight of our responsibility and opportunities to share that optimism with others. God told Abraham that He would bless him and that all the peoples on earth would be blessed *through him.* Being part of a Christian family is not a private corner on "the good life" but a special platform from which to demonstrate the reality of God.

Our children can grow up sensing that they are part of a team whose goal is to reach other people for Christ—a microcosmic prelude to what it means to be part of the Body of Christ.

Yet it starts with our perspective as parents. How can we expect our children to grow up with a burden and willingness to sacrifice for people in Africa if they don't see us reaching out to our neighborhood, to the people at the office, and to their friends?

Corrie Ten Boom's father, Casper, provides an amazing example of a man who not only ministered to people but also involved his family in that effort. In addition to his work for the Jews of Holland, he took care of ex-prisoners and their families. Also, an extraordinary group composed of agnostics, atheists, fundamentalists, a Calvinist, a liberal, and a Catholic met with him to study the book of Romans. As a result, Casper Ten Boom's children, by their late teens, were ministering to mentally retarded adults, to Jewish immigrants, and to soldiers.

Every Christian parent should ask, "What groups of people has God given me a burden for, an ability to work with, an open door to reach? How can I involve my children in an effort to reach these people?" John and Vera Perkins, who raised eight children in the midst of a thriving ministry in the black community, developed that ministry with their children in on the ground floor. Together with their children, John and Vera directed Good News Clubs in their neighborhood, and helped to establish a day care center and a thrift store.

For any family that ministers together, there is always a precarious tension between meeting the needs of the family and ministering to others. One layman shared with us his effort to maintain that balance. He scores himself weekly on a scale of a hundred, giving himself "points" for family devotional time, home projects, family recreational time, individual time with his children, and individual time with his wife. "Rarely do I hit a hundred," he says, "and certainly there is nothing sanctified about the list. But at least I have some measure of how well needs are being met within our family." Such a barometer provides a potential place to begin evaluating. It will not, however, answer the harder, more elusive questions, such as "Am I really in touch with my [wife or husband] or my children?" and "How well do I communicate warmth and love?"

We are preparing our children for a lifetime of walking with God and ministering to others. Jim Elliot wrote to his mother about this kind of preparation after he left home for Ecuador:

> Remember how the Psalmist described children? He said that they were as an heritage from the Lord, and that every man should be happy who had his quiver full of them. And what is a quiver full of but arrows? And what are arrows for but to shoot? So, with the strong arms of prayer, draw the bowstring back and let the arrows fly—all of them, straight at the Enemy's hosts.[4]

For some of us, there is no godly heritage to reflect on, no parent or grandparent who turned our eyes to the Lord. You might feel like the engineer of a huge locomotive racing down the mountainside, grinding the gears to bring you to a slow stop, and turning around to head back up the Mountain. Perhaps God wants to begin anew in your generation, to give you the privilege of being the first to pass on that Light to those to come.

Along with Moses, we should pray that God would give us a heart to fear Him and keep His commandments, that it might go well with us and with those who come after us.[6]

Notes

1. James Dobson, *Straight Talk to Men and Their Wives* (Waco: Word Books, 1980), pages 54-55.
2. Dobson, *Straight Talk*, page 49.
3. Lawrence Crabb, *Effective Biblical Counseling* (Grand Rapids: Zondervan, 1977), page 118.
4. Interview with J. Allan Petersen, conducted by Paula Rinehart in June 1985.
5. Elisabeth Elliot, *Shadow of the Almighty*, page 132.
6. See Deuteronomy 5:29.

11
The Ground of Our Hope

> Hope is the struggle of the soul, breaking loose from what is perishable and attesting her eternity.
>
> *Herman Melville*

October in Texas is summer's afterthought, its last hurrah before chill northern winds chase children indoors for jackets and hats. On one such pleasant afternoon Jason, his brother Asa, and their friend headed out for a bike ride after school.

As the sun was beginning to set on their play, Jason persuaded Asa to trade bikes for the return home. A few moments later, a truck driven by an angry, drunken man came speeding around the corner. He saw Asa too late to do anything but panic and jam on his brakes. His truck skidded off the road and hit Asa, who died within a few hours from massive internal injuries.

Jason, his parents, and their other two children were only beginning to put the pieces of life back together when, fifteen months later, Jason left for Colorado on a church youth ski trip.

Early one morning, after gaining confidence on some easier slopes, Jason and his friends decided to try a more difficult run. As he made his way down the slope, he came over a rise to find a lady standing in his path. He made a sudden swerve to miss her. Now he faced an obstacle even more ominous: the exposed roots of a tree. There wasn't time to turn again. He fell, hitting his head on the very object he had hoped to avoid. Three weeks later, Jason, who never regained consciousness, went to be with his brother and with the Lord.

The death of a child is said to be the ultimate loss, yet here was a family faced not with one but two such deaths within a span of months. What words of comfort could one offer to parents who sit before yet another son's casket, with crushing memories jogged so soon by the fragrance of funeral carnations?

Something tells us emphatically that this world was not meant to be like this. Some intuitive trace from the Garden, some profound dimension of our consciousness, leads us to recognize the terrible gap between what is and what should be. Those inscrutable caskets raise a thousand questions for which there are no simple answers. There is no how-to book or cherished formula to patch that kind of crack in the cosmos.

For most of us, life in a fallen world brings some measure of tragedy and heartache that cannot be explained, that cannot be chased away by the oversimplified exhortation to "have more faith." What are we to *do* when we ourselves are exposed to the ramifications of evil?

In *Book of the Dun Cow,* Walter Wangerin, Jr., symbolically portrays this enigma in a fantasy world with animals, over which the noble rooster Chauntecleer resides. The river, rumbling off in the distance, carries the dreaded serpents known as the Basilisks. As the story progresses, the river creeps closer and closer, an ominous presence that swells and overflows its banks, until eventually its serpents destroy Chauntecleer's own sons.

The illusion behind evil is that it exists only in some remote, terrorist-ridden place, another time zone removed. We feel safe enough to watch it from an easy chair on the six o'clock news, confident that the discord in the distance will leave us unscathed.

Then, with no warning, a measure of that evil invades our home. It is *our* brother who goes off to war, our child who is born brain-damaged. We watch helplessly as another person is given the promotion we deserve. One day we realize that the face needing a lift is the one greeting us in the morning mirror.

What remains for us is to decide how we will respond when the rains descend and the flood comes. What makes a godly response even more of a challenge in the face of evil is the distorted concept of God and His goodness that our culture portrays. Bad things are not supposed to happen to good people.

This gospel of prosperity can easily permeate, in varying degrees, our criteria for judging God's blessing upon our lives. To know that God has blessed us with every spiritual blessing and purchased eternal life for us is not enough. We also demand that He make life rewarding and pleasurable here and now. Against such a backdrop, we are doubly unprepared for unforeseen suffering or unexplainable tragedy.

This correlation between success and God's blessing has been brewing for a long time in American society. The Puritans considered hard work and piety to be natural outcomes of serving God. But eventually the traditional Puritan values of virtue, hard work, and piety became not an end in themselves but the means to the end of success. The abundant life promised by Christ has, in the long run, come to take the mutated shape of the prosperous American dream.

Writer and theologian Donald McCullough calls this the false ideal of the full cup—the idea that everything can and should be fullness and perfection in this life.[1] Such a common illusion produces a frustrating state of discontent riddled with "if onlys." If only my husband had a better job; if only I hadn't wrecked the car; if only we could have children . . . *then* life would be what it should be; the cup would be full.

The truth is that in a broken world we can never reach this false ideal of the full cup. Thus our spiritual maturity depends on whether or not we can learn how to live with unfulfillment.

Unless we see life from an eternal perspective, we will regard all material success as God's blessing and anything that makes life difficult as evidence of our failure or His disdain. We will chafe under whatever circumstances make life less pleasant.

The real gospel of prosperity

A close look at some of the major figures of Scripture presents us with a very different picture of what constitutes God's blessing. We marvel at the story of Peter's miraculous deliverance from jail (Acts 12:3-12). Yet only a few verses previous, we read matter-of-factly how Herod had James, the brother of John, put to death with the sword.

Is it not true that in God's eyes Peter and James were both delivered, both released—one in a literal sense and the other spiritually? And should the reality of being delivered into the presence of God be miraculous in any lesser way?

Or we might think of John the Baptist and all the celebration that accompanied his special birth. What a privilege was his to announce the way of the coming Messiah. His very name means "God is gracious." But if we judge the end of his life by the prevailing worldly views of success, how can we explain his waning popularity and his execution? Yet Jesus said of John that among those born of a woman, there was none greater (Matthew 11:11).

Perhaps the ultimate paradox is the life of Christ Himself. He reached the end of His life in the perfect will of God, watched His brothers turn against Him and His own people reject His Messiahship, and then died on a Roman cross between two thieves. If we were to apply the world's standards of success to His life, we would have to brand Him a pitiful failure.

We learn from Christ's life not that God always protects His children from evil but that He transforms the evil they encounter, bringing spiritual blessing out of the worst of fallen circumstances. The real gospel of prosperity lies not in the indulging of the body but in the testing of the soul. Even Jesus grew through trials.

> For whatever reason God chose to make man as he is—limited and suffering and subject to sorrows and death—He had the honesty and the courage to take His own medicine. Whatever game He is playing with His creation, He has kept His own rules and played fair. He can exact nothing from man that He has not exacted from Himself.[2]

Living with the mystery

Since even the Son of God learned obedience through what He suffered, do we dare think that we will somehow be exempt? The Good Shepherd suffered. His followers cannot expect to be lambs who are constantly petted and protected. Peter Marshall described this concept quite well:

> It is a fact of Christian experience that life is a series of troughs and peaks. In his efforts to get permanent possession of a soul, God relies on the troughs more than the peaks. And some of his special favorites have gone through longer and deeper troughs than anyone else.[3]

King David authored some of the most gripping devotional literature of the Bible. His psalms reveal the heart of a man totally given to seeking God. Some of his best psalms were written not from the luxurious, sheltered vantage of the palace but during his years on the run from Saul. "God is my stronghold," he wrote. "I know that [He] is for me. . . . O taste and see that the LORD is good" (Psalms 59:9, 56:9, 34:8). Here are words penned not in the cool confines of kingly life but in the midst of dodging spears, living in caves, and feigning insanity to save his neck. God used outward turmoil to spur David on in his inward journey toward holiness, thus forging steel in his soul.

God promises to use and transform the affliction He allows in our lives. It was this realization and conviction that caused Solzhenitsyn to say after ten years in a Soviet work camp, "I nourished my soul there, and I say without hesitation: '*Bless you, prison,* for having been in my life.'"[4] While lying on rotting prison straw, he realized for the first time that the foremost purpose of life is not prosperity, as we are often led to believe, but the maturing of the human soul. God is fitting us for eternity.

With our eyes fixed on that hope, we determine to serve God in prosperity *or* affliction. "Shall we indeed accept good from God," said Job, "and not accept adversity?" (Job 2:10). With these words Job unknowingly foiled Satan's attack upon him in the spiritual realm. Satan had boasted before the Lord that Job would jettison his faith like unwanted cargo once his wealth and family and health were taken away. "Does Job fear God for nothing?" Satan inquired sarcastically. In other words, "Of course he serves You; why wouldn't he? You've given him everything he could possibly want." But throughout his calamity, Job was resolute. He acknowledged that God had indeed given, and that God had taken away. God's character was not in question.

The phrase "God is good" cannot be reserved for those moments when life turns out the way we had hoped. Evangelist Leighton Ford spoke of how he wrestled with the meaning of that statement when his twenty-one-year-old son Sandy died following open-heart surgery: "Many times when someone says rather glibly, 'God answered this prayer; God did this miracle; God healed this person—isn't God good?' I've heard [my wife] say very quietly, 'Well, if God didn't heal, didn't do the miracle, is he not good?'" Of Sandy's death he added, "I don't understand it, but God *was* good."[5]

In the here and now, we must be content to live with questions only heaven will explain, trusting in the meantime that God is working out His eternal purposes beneath an intricate tapestry of mystery. When Paula and I lost a child through miscarriage at fourteen weeks, the doctor held up a small boy's limp form for us to see. "This baby was never meant to be," he said with the familiarity of one accustomed to such forever remembered moments. His comment was temporarily satisfying—that is, until the obvious reply formed itself: "If this baby was never meant to be, then why was it?"

There are few adequate answers this side of heaven for life's enigmas. There were none for Job. When God chose to respond to his dilemma, He offered not explanations but a series of sixty-six confounding questions. Job found peace, as any of us do, only by bowing in simple submission before the God whose judgments are unsearchable, whose ways are unfathomable (Romans 11:33).

What treasures eternity will hold as we see that intricate tapestry revealed with all the threads in perfect symmetry! Let us hasten to add that to turn our eyes toward heaven is no coward's effort to weasel out of struggling with the monumental questions of life. We struggle all right, but we also revel in the prospect of heaven's resolutions.

For the present, we must not insist that God pour out His blessings upon us in tangible, immediately gratifying ways. The ground of our hope cannot be found in the immediate, the here and now. Our hope, Peter reminds us, is that one day we will receive an inheritance that is imperishable, undefiled, and will not fade away (1 Peter 1:4). We establish our lives on that sure spiritual blessing. Even though it is unseen, it is quite real.

The difficulties of the present only make us stretch forward and squint our eyes with expectation, with hope of future fulfillment. *Then* we will experience a cup that is full and running over. Then we will see full face what we have heretofore only caught glimpses of in a mirror dimly.

As we experience the many simple pleasures of this life—the slobbery kiss of an exuberant toddler, a walk on a deserted beach, the lemony smell of old wood restored—we know they are foretastes of the joy of eternity. But our expectations for fulfillment must lie in the substance of the future, not the shadows of the present.

This world—fallen, rebellious, and groaning for release—is on a collision course with disaster. The ship is going down. No amount of positive thinking, helpful seminars, or teeth-gritting determination can permanently prevent the river from rising. And while, as C. S. Lewis said, we relish the "fine irony" of keeping the ship in order, we know the destiny of that ship.

Our hope is in the Lord. Someday we will shake off our mortality just as an insect abandons his cocoon. As C. S. Lewis put it, all earthly experiences will fade, "not as a candle flame that is put out, but as a candle flame that becomes invisible because someone has pulled up the blind, thrown open the shutters, and let in the blaze of the risen sun."

Notes

1. Donald McCullough, "The Pitfalls of Positive Thinking," *Christianity Today* (September 6, 1985), pages 23-24.
2. Dorothy Sayers, *A Matter of Eternity* (Grand Rapids: Eerdmans, 1973), page 30.
3. Peter Marshall, *Leadership Journal* (Spring 1984), page 97.
4. Aleksandr Solzhenitsyn, *The Gulag Archipelago, II*, page 615.
5. Leighton Ford, "Yes, God is Good," *Decision Magazine* (June 1982), page 5.

12
Is It Worth It?

> He who provides for this life but takes no care for eternity is wise for a moment but a fool forever.
>
> *John Tillotson*

I spent my girlhood years nestled in the Blue Ridge Mountains of Virginia in a house perched on a mountainside, shaded by two-hundred-year-old oak trees. From my bedroom window, I could see out across the hills of New River Valley, hills that were French-knotted by pink dogwoods in the spring and rolls of hay in the summer. Ridge after mountain ridge framed the sky in shadowy coats of blue. For more than twenty years, I awoke to the same view from the same window. Unknowingly, I was sinking roots down as deep as those of the old oaks.

Eventually I was married, and within two days after the wedding Stacy and I were heading out in a one-way Ryder truck bound for Texas. We have been moving west ever since, from one wind-blown plain to another. At this time in our lives, we wake up to the stark, masculine beauty of the Rockies.

Occasionally I board a plane, and within three hours, I am standing there surrounded by those old familiar hills again. Without any conscious thought, a feeling sweeps over me, reminding me that I am home. I know this place; it is part of me.

And then, with a startling realization, I am jerked from my trance. No, this is not home—not if I believe what the Bible tells me. In the truest sense, home is heaven. Yet when I arrive in heaven, I fully expect to experience that old recognizable feeling I sometimes have for the Blue Ridge Mountains. The feeling is a legitimate one. But for a long time I mistook the ultimate object of that attraction.

What I will know when I arrive home in heaven, without even having to think about it, is that this is where and what and Who I was made for. I belong there.

Coming home. Is there any more inviting way of looking at heaven, that future world where we will spend eternity directly, personally with the Lord? Is there any more comforting thought than realizing that we will experience our fellowship with Him far more purely, having been purged of our lazy, corrupt flesh? Our will shall be free to obey perfectly, for then "it can do what it likes, for it cannot but like what it ought."[1]

If we would allow ourselves to think more of that homecoming, perhaps the struggles and discomforts of the present would fade into reticent shadows by comparison. One of the enemy's favorite ploys has always been to convince us that God will accept our effort and sacrifice, but will leave us shortchanged.

Toward the beginning of the twentieth century, Henry Morrison, the president of Asbury College, left on an evangelistic tour of China under the auspices of the Methodist Church. After weeks of arduous living and a demanding schedule, he and his wife were at last returning aboard a ship bound for the States, greatly in need of rest and encouragement.

This would prove to be no ordinary trip on an ocean liner, however. President Teddy Roosevelt was on board, returning from an African safari. When the ship entered the harbor, cheering crowds lined the docks hoping for a glimpse of the president. But there was no one there to greet the Morrisons.

The contrast was too much for Henry Morrison to assimilate. After all, he had given himself in service to a much higher cause than that of Roosevelt the hunter. There he was—forced to wade through a shoulder-to-shoulder crowd assembled for a man who had just returned from hunting elephants! Was such sacrifice and humiliation even worth it? But just at that point, when he was tempted to give in to bitterness and discouragement, his wife stopped him short with this rejoinder: "But, Henry, you aren't Home yet."

You don't have to be a returning missionary to struggle with the question, "Is it worth it to follow God?" Over four hundred years before Christ, Malachi recorded that God's people complained, "It is vain to serve God; and what profit is it that we have kept His charge . . . ?" (Malachi 3:14).

Perhaps this is why Scripture repeats with such forcefulness the theme that God will reward His children for their faithfulness. It is His nature to give. Jesus told His followers, "Do not be afraid, little flock, for your Father has chosen gladly to give you the kingdom" (Luke 12:32). Even when men mistreat us because of the gospel, we are to "be glad in that day, and leap for joy, for behold, [our] reward is great in heaven" (Luke 6:23).

Although we should never think of the Bible as an advertising catalog giving detailed descriptions of luxurious rewards in heaven, there are crowns promised for those who overcome the flesh, lead others to Christ, endure trials, and shepherd God's flock. There is even a crown for those who long for Christ's return. Notice that the eternal prize always seems to require the sacrifice of some temporal prize. Jesus mentioned "treasures in heaven" to the rich young man as the eternal result of giving his earthly treasure to the poor.

Though most of the scriptural language describing rewards in heaven is veiled and mysterious, one thing is clear: Not only will we be with Christ, but we will be *like* Him. That in itself would seem like enough. But God also promises that each of us will have some official position or job in His Kingdom. And with a wealth of imagery, we are told that we will have "glory."

Yet ironically, in spite of how insistently the Bible mentions future eternal rewards, Christians seem to rarely broach the subject. The first major reason for our hesitancy is that the topic has a potentially odd, mercenary feel to it. We don't want to appear to have the wrong motives. Someone might think that we consider knowing God for eternity to be secondary to receiving His trophies. The second reason is that we tend to shy away from any reminder of eternal accountability for the stewardship of our earthly life.

Both of these mind-sets reveal confusion and misunderstanding about what God is saying in Scripture. C. S. Lewis addressed this question of whether the desire to experience God's praise and reward is an impure motivation:

> No one can enter heaven except as a child; and nothing is so obvious in a child . . . as its great and undisguised pleasure in being praised. . . . When the redeemed soul . . . learns at last that she has pleased Him whom she was created to please . . . there will be no room for vanity then. She will be free from the miserable illusion that it is her doing.[2]

Our desire to experience God's glory—His praise and rewards—expresses our confidence in His character and our conviction that the future will hold in full what we know now only in part. It is no mercenary aspiration. Christ Himself *for the joy set before Him* endured the Cross and despised its shame (Hebrews 12:2). He didn't belittle the discomfort, or call pain "pleasure." He faced death by setting His eyes upon the sure hope of sitting eternally at the right hand of the Father.

Our longing to experience heaven's glories and rewards is a valid indication that we were made for another world.

> Our lifelong nostalgia, our longing to be reunited with something in the universe from which we now feel cut off, to be on the inside of some door which we have always seen from the outside, is no mere neurotic fancy, but the truest index of our real situation.[3]

But heaven will also contain some measure of accountability for the life we now live. "For we must all appear before the judgment-seat of Christ, that each one may be recompensed for his deeds in the body, according to what he has done, whether good or bad" (2 Corinthians 5:10). It is not really condemnation that we hear in this verse. It is simply a reminder that since Jesus Christ is our eternal foundation, we should each determine how to build on that eternal security here and now. Someday the fire of God will reveal the quality of our work, leaving either a morass of stubble or something worthy and permanent. Every thought, attitude, and action will be evaluated. Everything in this life, mysteriously enough, takes on meaning in light of eternity. What we do now has eternal consequences.

One of the hidden rhythms of the universe is

the principle that we reap what we sow. The person who gives himself wholeheartedly to Christ's service here and now consequently knows more of the joy of the Lord. The Bible gives us no warrant for thinking that it will be different in heaven.

Christ told many parables illustrating stewardship. In one, the nobleman gave each person the same amount of money; in another, each received a different amount of money, "according to his ability." In both cases, Christ clearly commended those who were faithful with the opportunities and resources they were given. Those who squandered their resources were severely rebuked.

Paul freely admitted that the reality of standing before God and experiencing the review of his life motivated him to live uncompromisingly for God. Perhaps if we allowed ourselves to contemplate heaven, to actually picture ourselves standing before the Lord in the future, then eternity would dictate more of our choices and ambitions in the present. For, indeed, we are forging right now our capacity to appreciate the Lord for all eternity. We are polishing the mirrors with which we will reflect His glory forever.

Thy Kingdom come

For over two full centuries now, men and women have stood to the strains of the "Hallelujah Chorus" from Handel's *Messiah*: "For the Lord God omnipotent reigneth. The kingdom of this world is become the kingdom of our Lord, and of His Christ; and He shall reign forever and ever." When we hear those words, it is as if the veil is pulled aside and we glimpse the world as it really is, and really will be: one where Christ reigns forever as Lord. Handel was found in tears after he finished composing the *Messiah*, saying, "I did think I saw all heaven before me, and the great God Himself."

It is that exhilarating melody of the Promised Land that enables us to dance even now. Our choices in life will mirror for us where our hope lies and whether we really hear that melody. Only a preoccupation with this greater glory will remove the lust, pride, and carnal ambition that plagues us in the present.

To adopt an eternal perspective is to see life as the Bible presents it: from the end, as though the future overlaid the present.

> This view separates what is real from what is unreal. What is real is what will last. Everything else, no matter how real it seems to us, is treated as insubstantial, hardly worth a snort. That is why Scripture can seem at times so blithely and irritatingly out of touch with reality, brushing past huge philosophical problems and personal agony. That is just how life is, when you are looking from the end. Perspective changes everything.[4]

As Paul said, "I consider that the sufferings of this present time are not worthy to be compared with the glory that is to be revealed to us" (Romans 8:18). We are like the woman who writhes in the pain and labor of childbirth. She does not despair. She knows that shortly, in the near future, she will hold a crying, vibrant child: the benefit of her discomfort.

To settle for a halfhearted, compromising walk with God in this life would be to enter His presence shrinking back in shame. We want to live for God now in such a way that will bring us enjoyable fruits for all eternity. "Godliness is profitable for all things . . . for the present life and also for the life to come" (1 Timothy 4:8).

We will not be fully at home until we dwell in heaven with the Lord. C. S. Lewis describes the tide of hope that carries us toward our eternal haven, and the kind of effect that tide should have on our lives:

> If we consider . . . the staggering nature of the rewards promised in the Gospels, it would seem that our Lord finds our desires, not too strong, but too weak. We are half-hearted creatures, fooling about with drink and sex and ambition when infinite joy is offered us, like an ignorant child who wants to go on making mud pies in a slum because he cannot imagine what is meant by the offer of a holiday at the sea. We are far too easily pleased.

We have God's Word that all our effort and travail now will be eternally worth it: "Eye hath not see, nor ear heard, neither have entered into the heart of man, the things which God hath prepared for them that love him" (1 Corinthians 2:9, KJV).

Notes

1. Dorothy Sayers, *A Matter of Eternity* (Grand Rapids: Eerdmans, 1973), page 81.
2. C. S. Lewis, *The Weight of Glory*, page 9.
3. C. S. Lewis, *The Weight of Glory*, page 12.
4. Tim Stafford, "The Age to Come," *Christianity Today* (May 17, 1985), page 32.

13
A New Order

The people who hanged Christ never, to do them justice, accused Him of being a bore—on the contrary; they thought Him too dynamic to be safe.

Dorothy Sayers

Jesus Christ represents the entrance of eternity into history. God slipped unobtrusively into the stream of human events, being born the same year that Caesar Augustus took a census for taxes. No fanfare announced the arrival of this peasant couple's baby, yet history turned a corner at His coming.

His life was like none other, before or after. A man of contrasts, Jesus healed broken bodies, but exposed the sickness of the soul. He dined with unorthodox sinners, but rattled the cages of religious traditionalists. His presence drew crowds, drove out demons, and divided families. He brought both comfort and consternation.

Groups of disciples and curious onlookers

would stand with their mouths gaping open, astonished and confounded by His teaching. In His Kingdom, the last would be first, the one who saved his life would lose it, the righteous beggar would be comforted in heaven while the rich man would languish in the fires of hell. His best known sermon contained a series of reversals: "You have heard it said . . . but I say to you. . . ." Clearly, He came to establish a radical new order.

"My kingdom is not of this world," He said, and His followers nodded their heads in agreement (John 18:36). Surely His Kingdom looked upside-down, unlike anything they had seen before.

One area of almost total incomprehension surfaced repeatedly in various contexts: the definition of greatness. In the Gospels we see Christ and His disciples traveling on the way to Jerusalem only one week before His death. For the third time He was now telling them in plain terms that He must be delivered up to the chief priests and scribes to be condemned to death. But His disciples could not understand, nor did it seem that they even cared to. No specter of a cross was hanging before their vision. This was the Messiah, and Jerusalem was the place where they were expecting Him to come into the glory of His Kingdom.

James and John were the first to voice their aspirations aloud: "Grant that we may sit in Your glory, one on Your right, and one on Your left" (Mark 10:37). The other ten seemed to be indignant that James and John got to Jesus first with a request for positions of honor and power.

Strangely enough, Jesus did not reprimand them for seeking greatness and significance. He did, however, point in a different direction to show them the means of reaching their goal: In His Kingdom, the one who would be great must be, first of all, the greatest of servants. The way up was down. Even the One who was rightfully King, before whose feet men might justly fall, came as a servant to suffer and die.

We should not be discouraged if we fail to grasp all that Jesus was saying here. His disciples certainly didn't grasp it. Peter, one of those closest to Jesus, vacillated back and forth between unusual courage and insight, and the thickest of spiritual denseness. When Jesus asked His disciples who they thought He was, it was Peter who answered, "Thou art the Christ, the Son of the living God" (Matthew 16:16). This radical statement indicated that Peter was willing to turn his back on his Jewish religion and culture. Had he been among a crowd of Pharisees at the time, they would probably have stoned him for blasphemy.

Yet when Jesus then began to speak of His mission of death and suffering, Peter took Him aside to rebuke the mere suggestion. After all, Jesus had just promised to give him the keys of His Kingdom. Who could wish for a special position in a slain leader's defaulted domain?

Christ's strong, severe words, "Get behind Me, Satan!" revealed His abhorrence toward anything that reeked of self-seeking and self-protection. Peter apparently did not understand the ways of Jesus' Kingdom, for his first thought was for his own interests. But in the Kingdom of God, the cross always precedes the crown (Luke 9:23-24, 14:27).

So, ironically, greatness in God's upside-down Kingdom is a combination of selflessness and servanthood. This is so antithetical to all we observe and are taught in society that it's easy to dismiss Christ's words, as His disciples did, as the utopian ideals of a Man unacquainted with "the real world." Jesus obviously had read nothing about assertiveness training or winning through intimidation. What would He have to say about the Christian community today, where our heroes are no longer the saints and the servants but rather the entrepreneurs and the celebrities, whose faith is generously underscored with wealth, position, and good fortune?

How do we apply the uncompromising message of Jesus in this modern, corporate world, where many a company president addresses his assembled employees like this: "Monday through Friday you belong to me—body, mind, and soul. Weekends are yours to rest and think about how you can do a better job and advance in this company"? Employees who have any hope of promotion generally give twelve hours a day to that endeavor. The competitive work environment is structured to spur each person on in his mad scramble to advance.

We live and work in a world whose system we, as followers of Christ, have intrinsically repudiated. To apply what Christ taught about greatness is to resist the temptation to sell yourself, to advance at the cost of another's downfall, to be your own public relations man. Living in Christ's Kingdom entails a completely different approach: a willingness to make my boss, my staff, and my associates look good.

Sometimes in my devotional time, I find myself praying, "Lord, I am *Your* servant." But I no sooner get the words out of my mouth than the faces of those closest to me pass before my mind's eye: my wife, my children, those I work with. I can sense the Lord responding, in effect, "That's fine. It's wonderful that you are My servant. But will you serve Me by serving *them*?"

When you think of achieving "greatness"—and we all do at times—do you imagine Jesus asking you, as He asked Peter and John, "Are you willing, then, to lay aside the world's criteria for greatness, nullifying your own selfish interests? Are you willing to come as a servant?"

At the heart of this new order

Christ's task on earth was to accomplish the mission of salvation. He could have gone to the Cross with a soldier's attitude toward duty, an engineer's objective assessment of the need of the moment. But we cannot read the New Testament and fail to see the heart of the Father revealed in the Son. The nature of Christ's Kingdom is most expressly revealed in His heart for people.

Jesus loved the people He came to save. His love was not the patronizing charity of one person who condescends to help another, but the self-effacing heart of one who could be touched with the feeling of our infirmities. Here was someone who would blatantly incur the wrath of the Pharisees in order to heal a man's hand, elevating the person above the religious system. As Christ touched the ostracized leper, He healed far more than his physical affliction. Jesus expressed His love by embracing children, whose worth in the Jewish culture was measured only by their lineage. Moreover, He even declared children to be *models* of His Kingdom.

Perhaps the heart of Jesus was most evident in the extension of His ministry to the multitudes, who, at some points, seemed to follow Him everywhere. The feeding of the five thousand took place just when the exhausted disciples were in need of rest and retreat. Jesus and His men had set out for a lonely place, but the multitudes ran ahead and met them, making their arrival anything but lonely. It was the equivalent of planning a weekend away, and arriving at your destination only to discover that the people you just left behind had gotten there first.

But Jesus was not irritated. He looked at the multitudes and saw a mass of desperate people with nowhere to turn, sheep without a shepherd. He began to teach them, and by and by served dinner to more than five thousand. Some of these people would eventually be there to lend a sympathetic hand at the scene of His death.

Christ's compassion is even more amazing when we consider that He truly knew what was in people's hearts. He could see with three-dimensional clarity the evil we only faintly glimpse. It is His example above all that provides the staying power in any personal attempt to spiritually shepherd others. We have, on one hand, the knowledge that a person might radically disappoint us, and on the other, the hope that Christ's touch might heal the inward desolation and make that person fully what he was meant to be.

Coming on His terms

The eternal life offered by Jesus has its own particular charisma and drawing power. His Kingdom appeals to man's highest and noblest aspirations. In Him we recognize the substance of what we have always longed for, the fulcrum on which our lives can balance.

Christ offered the warmest of invitations to His Kingdom: the prospect of rest for all who were weary, and living water for the spiritually thirsty. He welcomed with open arms anyone who would come to Him. But in the warmth of that reception, He never disguised the reality of the Cross. He never lowered the standards.

Jesus said that His followers should anticipate the rootless existence of a pilgrim. Jesus Himself had nowhere to lay His head. He informed His would-be disciples that there were no legitimate excuses for delay. He would not even permit a prospective disciple to return to say good-by to his family (Luke 9:57-62). Why? Because Christ's claims on one's life supersede every other responsibility. There is no room for looking back at what you have left behind, thereby devaluing the more worthy treasure of God's Kingdom.

Jesus felt a love for the rich young man who

approached Him, and longed to give him what he lacked. Yet the man, for all his outward righteousness, clung inwardly to his wealth. Jesus made it clear that God could fill only empty hands.

Christ's requirements for following Him cut across the grain of every human affection. We cannot read the accounts in Scripture honestly without a slight intake of breath. Every person in the New Testament who truly responded to Him was radically changed from the encounter. It cannot be less for us.

Of all those people, Matthew was one of the most interesting. He was obviously a well-educated man with an astute business sense. His name meant "Son of Levi." Some historians suggest that his was a religious upbringing. At one time he might have carried out Levitical duties in the temple.

But Matthew was also a man of opportunity. He overthrew any nagging religious or patriotic scruples to become a detested but successful tax collector. Rome required only a fixed percentage of Matthew's levy, leaving him free to size up his victims and charge whatever he could leech from his prey. Matthew's tax-collecting business for Rome was on the road to Capernaum, not far from where Peter and the other fishermen lived. In fact, he probably had some business dealings with Jesus Himself.

Perhaps the nagging dissatisfaction of realizing that what he had would not purchase what he wanted made Matthew particularly receptive to Jesus. At any rate, when Jesus passed by his tax office and said, "Follow Me," Matthew arose immediately and followed.

Matthew, probably more than any other disciple, was forced to make a complete, immediate severance with the past. He even invited his tax-collector friends to a dinner with Jesus, thereby openly identifying with Him and safeguarding his commitment. He would not follow from afar in secret. Matthew went on to become a biographer of Jesus. We owe him our gratitude for disclosing the largest portion of the Sermon on the Mount. As a former cutthroat businessman, he was quick to acknowledge the truth of Jesus' words that, indeed, man cannot serve both God and money.

Disciples like Matthew who left without hesitation to follow Jesus are never spoken of in the New Testament in heroic overtones. Theirs was simply the logical response of anyone who has some faint glimmer of the Life that Jesus offers. That's why Jesus never volunteered to lower His standards for following Him. The prize of the Kingdom itself is so infinitely worth whatever the cost. How can you compare trading a fishing boat for a throne?

"The kingdom of heaven," Jesus said, "is like a merchant seeking fine pearls, and upon finding one pearl of great value, he went and sold all that he had, and bought it" (Matthew 13:45-46). You can imagine a man who has dealt in the trading of pearls for years suddenly coming across the pearl of all pearls—a pearl of such quality that he sells all he has to possess it. His is an almost irrational abandonment, which is at once the sanest of responses. Nothing in his possession is even mildly comparable to that Pearl.

It was this fundamental truth that was in view when Jesus challenged His disciples to consider the seriousness of the commitment to follow Him. Peter spoke as the representative of all true believers when he responded, "Lord, to whom shall we go? You have words of eternal life" (John 6:68). Who else—what else—will we turn to? He is the Pearl.

It is one of the tragicomic ironies of life that Christ's Kingdom, which appears to be so upside-down in this world, is, in fact, right-side-up. What the world sees as normal is, from an eternal perspective, quite abnormal. It is only in light of eternity that we can see which is the counterfeit and which is the reality.